EDWARD BOND

LETTERS

I

D1610869

Contemporary Theatre Studies

A series of books edited by Franc Chamberlain, Nene College, Northampton, UK

Please see the back of this book for other titles in the Contemporary Theatre Studies series.

EDWARD BOND

LETTERS

I

Selected and edited
by
Ian Stuart
University of Southern California, Los Angeles, USA

harwood academic publishers
Australia • Canada • China • France • Germany • India •
Japan • Luxembourg • Malaysia • The Netherlands • Russia •
Singapore • Switzerland • Thailand • United Kingdom

Amsteldijk 166
1st Floor
1079 LH Amsterdam
The Netherlands

Library of Congress Cataloging-in-Publication Data

Bond, Edward.
    [Correspondence]
    Edward Bond letters / selected and edited by Ian Stuart.
        p.   cm, — (Contemporary theatre studies: V. 5)
    Includes index.
    ISBN 3-7186-5504-7
    1. Bond, Edward—Correspondence.   2. Dramatists, English—20th
century—Correspondence.   I. Stuart, Ian, 1962– .   II. Title.
III. Title: Letters.   IV. Series.
PR6052.05Z48   1993
822'.914 — dc20
    [B]

93-46284
CIP

CONTENTS

Chapter Four   Productions

INTRODUCTION TO THE SERIES

Contemporary Theatre Studies is a book series of special interest to everyone involved in theatre. It consists of monographs on influential figures, studies of movements and ideas in theatre, as well as primary material consisting of theatre-related documents, performing editions of plays in English, and English translations of plays from various vital theatre traditions worldwide.

Franc Chamberlain

PREFACE

Beginning in the 1980s Edward Bond's dissociation with the established theatre was inevitable as many leading theatres, such as the RSC and the Royal National Theatre, produced plays antithetical to his belief in a new and useful theatre. Consequently, most of Bond's latest plays were not staged in London but given performances in the regions or abroad. This separation from the London theatre as a venue for his latest work along with Bond's interest in other European productions has resulted in a number of letters written to students and theatre professionals to explain and comment on the plays. The present collection is a selection of these letters.

Edward Bond Letters Volume I is organised into four chapters. In these letters Bond discusses his approach to acting and directing; theatre events (TEs); politics; and recent productions of his work. Subsequent volumes will focus more specifically on the plays and translations.

Edward Bond was born and educated in London. His plays included *The Pope's Wedding* (Royal Court Theatre, 1962), *Saved* (Royal Court, 1965), *Early Morning* (Royal Court, 1968), *Narrow Road to the Deep North* (Belgrade Theatre, Coventry, 1968; Royal Court, 1969), *Black Mass* (Sharpeville Commemoration Evening, Lyceum Theatre, 1970), *Passion* (CND Rally, Alexandra Palace, 1971), *Lear* (Royal Court, 1971), *The Sea* (Royal Court, 1973), *Bingo* (Northcott, Exeter, 1973; Royal Court, 1974), *The Fool* (Royal Court, 1975), *The Bundle* (RSC Warehouse, 1978), *The Woman* (National Theatre, 1978), *The Worlds* (New Half Moon Theatre, London, 1981), *Restoration* (Royal Court, 1981), *Summer* (National Theatre, 1982), *Derek* (RSC Youth Festival, The Other Place, Stratford-upon-Avon, 1982), *The Cat* (produced in Germany as *The English Cat* by the Stuttgart Opera, 1983), *Human Cannon* (Quantum Theatre, Manchester, 1986), *The War Plays* (*Red Black and Ignorant, The Tin Can People,* and *Great Peace* staged as a trilogy in Holland and Portugal, 1987), *September* (Canterbury Cathedral, 1989), *In the Company of Men* (Paris, 1992), *Jackets* (Paris, 1993), *Olly's Prison* (BBC Television, 1993; first stage production, Paris,

1993), *Tuesday* (BBC Schools Television, 1993). Bond's *Theatre Poems and Songs* were published in 1978 and *Poems 1978–1985* in 1987.

A word about punctuation. Edward Bond has his own unique style of punctuation which I have tried to preserve. I have also provided footnotes which will refer the reader to published texts and, I hope, clarify references.

ACKNOWLEDGMENTS

I am very grateful to Edward Bond for granting me permission to publish these letters and for correcting my typographical errors. My thanks to Elisabeth Bond-Pablé and also Tom Erhardt of Casarotto Ramsay Limited for his help. The School of Theatre at the University of Southern California has been very generous in providing research assistance. My gratitude to Jennifer Nichols, Renee Bade, and, especially, Jeffrey Flint without whose dedication and patience these volumes would never have been completed. I have received excellent publication advice from Robert Robertson, Valerie Rose, and Oona Campbell. Finally, I would like to express appreciation to my parents who have followed my work with enthusiasm.

Ian Stuart
Los Angeles, California
December 1993

LIST OF PRINCIPAL CORRESPONDENTS

Moshen Baraket, former student, University of Kent, Canterbury, 1990

John Clemo, writer, 1990

Ruby Cohn, Professor, University of California, Davis

Mark Ellis, a director of a production of *Narrow Road to the Deep North*

Michael Fuller, Adjunct Assistant, School of Theatre, University of Southern California

David Jansen, former student, Royal Holloway and Bedford New College, 1989

Nigel Jamieson, International Workshop Festival, 1989

Ria Julian, theatre director, Hungary, 1988

Calum MacCrimmon, former student, Worcester College of Higher Education, 1989

Benjamin May, former student, Lancaster University, 1992

Adrian Noble, currently artistic director, Royal Shakespeare Company

Max Stafford-Clark, former artistic director, Royal Court Theatre

Ian Stuart, editor, University of Southern California

Oleg Yefremov, International Stanislavsky Centre, Moscow, 1989

Chapter One

Acting and Directing

Michael Fuller

Hollywood, California   13 January 1988

Dear Mr. Fuller,

Thank you for your letter in which you tell me that you are preparing a production of *The Sea*.[1] I will try to comment on the points you make in your letter. Of course it's difficult to comment on acting in this way. It would be easier to demonstrate. Against that, having to write forces one to define and generalise, and that is clearly useful. On the other hand, how much worse off we would be if we had only Brecht's written theories and the comments of his earlier collaborators (Lotte Lenya: "Brecht never spoke about his theories - they didnt matter in rehearsal.") without the priceless examples of his Berliner Ensemble productions.

You say that the actor's job is to discover the character within himself and that the director's job is to arrange the performances and put them into some sort of epic framework. Of course, I'm manipulating what you say into a contentious paraphrase - but it's not too unfair: where you wish to get outside these restrictive but supportive confines you become vaguer. You say (I quote): "the actors tap emotional reality. They expose it. At the height of the exposure - the zenith of nakedness, they comment upon it; they dance it; they sound-movement it; they laugh at it - point at it - THIS objectifies it. The staging is pictorial-symbolic - a physical manifestation of an idea, a theme."

---

[1] Michael Fuller directed <u>The Sea</u> with MFA acting students at the University of Southern California, Los Angeles, Spring 1988.

This is nonsense - but attractive nonsense for which I have a lot of sympathy but no tolerance... It needs to be worked on. You say: "(epic) requires the actor to make the same personal commitments in Realism, but then to comment on it instead of act it out." You also say: "Actors work to tap emotional reality... They bring characters out of themselves... all characters already exist within one, and have to, since one has been 5 or so."

This suggests that people work on themselves in the way *you* suggest a director works on characters - and this seems to me the basis of a profound misunderstanding. Some time ago I had a letter from someone in the drama department of the University of California, in which at a critical moment he switched from an argument about an event on the stage (a rape) to the same event on the street - and argued as if there were a continuity of subject.[2] This is probably due to the same basic mistake.

Clearly not all characters can exist in an infant and equally clearly reactions to a stage rape are not the same as to those of a street rape (at the most naive level, we dont warn Gertrude the cup is poisoned - but we do shout rape when we see it on the street). So there isnt a continuity between stage and reality in a naive sense. Suppose Im born in 1890 and in 1914 I have to portray a young first world war pilot: how could that character exist in me in 1895 - aeroplanes hadnt been invented. But the inventor of aeroplanes had? No - flight *may* have been impossible by physical laws - it happened not to be - and so the inventors didnt exist in 1895: they existed merely retrospectively when certain laws of aerodynamics were discovered. This may seem a pedantic point, but I hope to make clear why it isnt: when the physical laws were incorporated into human reality, the human condition changed. So you'd have to argue that of course characters dont exist in infants, but that potentials do - no doubt characteristic universals in humans, such as the ability to feel angry, to laugh, to speak a language, to fall in love, etc.

My argument is this - and I dont want to fully argue this philosophically here because it would require a too long excursus, though I certainly think the argument is possible. So instead I'll say it's better if we proceed as if what I say were true - because this would enable us to tackle the problems of acting practically and fruitfully. The philosophical problems are in any case complex. Suppose like Chomsky you argue that there are in the mind innate grammatical

---

2 Letter from Editor, Fall 1987.

structures which are then filled by a learned language - so that the structures can be filled by German, Latin, etc. - and that the third angle of the triangle consists in the learned-language's practicality in the real world (it enables the character to live). Here the innate structure is ghost-like - in physical terms, a structure without shape (if that's imaginable). A structure with only abstract characteristics - like an invisible wall of glass controlling egress and ingress. Practical reality (the world in which we speak about the world and our actions in order to live) then (as it were) paints a picture onto this glass-screen - though you have to think of a content - in passing: the philosophical blur is then how did they get there since they would seem to be outside normal evolutionary disciplines - but there are possible answers: think of the structures as extendibles (as, say, elements of mathematics) or like those little curled comic toys children have - you blow into them and they unroll, extend, with your breath and - into the bargain - make a funny screech! You couldnt operate on the infant's head and find the spoken language electronically coded in the synapses of its brain prior to learning - as you could learned experience. (Though the mechanical techniques for this sort of exploration are crude and limited, they are still available for elementary exploration). So reality, experience, has to give content to an abstract ability. And if a child didnt hear a speaker (as with deaf children and - it's said - abandoned children later found as adults) they wouldnt learn a language - the innate structures in the mind (at least in so far as they are not merely aspects of other intellectuating abilities, such as that of discerning continuity in varying shapes) would remain sterile, dead, have no presence.

But you are talking of characteristics which are precisely the opposite: anger, joy, etc have an absolute, existential existence which is part of the "presence of reality" - and just as a chair must exist before people name it, so joy, sadness etc exist before people can experience them - indeed such emotions are seen as inductors and corrigents of human experience, indeed as given elements in consciousness. So a baby sucks the nipple because it is hungry? - but who taught it that hunger *is* desire for food and that you fulfill a need by ingesting milk from a breast? It seems obvious because it's simple and even a baby can do it! - but actually it has to be learned - and in a way is even more complex - than going into a restaurant, reading a menu, using cutlery, counting money and calculating a tip in such a way as to show a mental attitude towards a state of physical repletion or perhaps annoyance. The relation between hunger and feeding is learned. It's pre-language learning, and all infants that survive infancy learn the same lesson - but it puts learning (the structure of the world with cause-and-effect) at the most basic level of human experience. A child that experiences hunger isnt human - any more than a stone on which the wind howls is sighing. What makes the infant human is that it learns a lesson: it connects hunger with repletion and learns what to do. The lesson becomes a boundary of its humanity - as integral and foreign to it as its skin. It is defined by the lesson, it learns learning. Soon of course it will learn to use learnings as weapons (you could refer to my argument about tools and weapons in *Human Cannon* to see this working in extended social and political structures). There is an idea that there is an innate mushy human nature which has somehow to be trained, coerced and repressed in order to turn the little animal into a human being. Supposing you walk in a field and there are lumps of clay everywhere. You dont point at them and say: what badly made pots. A pot is a structure created by a human being who has been taught by a culture. Only with the culture does pottery become possible and (as technology imposes its pressure on the community) necessary. So is say an emotion like joy an abstraction which is put into a context - thus forming an intermediate instance between abstract language structures and idealistic notions of a pre-given soul?

For our present purpose we need to say only that emotions only exist in context. This seems a banal conclusion after the argument so far. But it's a vital point. Emotions arent emotions! - but statements. Imagine an old-fashioned printer's work-bench: there is his tray of metal letters which he can form into words and lines. The letters exist prior to the use of them in printing. We think of emotions in this way - and it's a mistaken way of thinking. The emotions dont pre-exist: the letters are created by the words. Or imagine a book which says: I intend to learn the alphabet and thus become a more interesting book - that's a more exact description of the humanising process. For humans, the letters dont create the words and sentences - but vice versa. There isnt an innate, existential, feeling, emoting self: the self is created by intellectuations. My quarrel with Brecht is that he probably has a seventeenth century, Cartesian attitude to mind which saw a radical distinction between feelings and emotions on the one hand and reason on the other. But to think about a social problem is to disentangle badly written lines - and you cant cut off emotions from meanings anymore than you can cut off the tides from the sea. In practice, of course, Brecht certainly acknowledges this - there couldnt be any human communication without this acknowledgement.

The oddity about the human brain is that it has a capacity infinitely beyond its apparent needs. A primitive culture may count on its fingers - and may perhaps count no further than three. For the members of a culture to be able to do this means that the whole of mathematics is possible for them, as a process of cultural discoveries (an obvious example is the Islamic creation of algebra). Yet the human mind - once it can observe the practicality of its hands - observes that cause-and-effect is a general truth (practically) - will immediately apply this lesson to everything: so the most primitive communities speculate about the nature of the stars and the changes of the seasons and the content of darkness etc. even when they can only count to three - no other animal does this, it merely acquires isolated skills which it cannot generalise into a philosophy - it never asks questions - merely (at most) confronts enigmas which the world forcibly presents to it. This human oddity means that reality is explained long before it's understood. The explanations arent random but rigidly confined: they relate the individual to his society, they explain society as a projection of the cosmos (god or something like that). This is true of adults: they necessarily imagine a reality and necessarily act accordingly. This isnt to say that eighteenth century Puritans are filled with hate and they must discharge it on witches: the belief in witches is a product of society, of its ideas - and the ideas create fear. So in witch-crazes we dont see the old Adam, the ancient human nature, rearing its ugly head: we see the ideas of an advanced, increasingly more civilized, technically capable society, an *increasingly scientific* society (it's important), responding to misunderstood facts: I can make a machine work in an orderly way - presumably the devil must be creating such disorder and hysteria in these women. We always interpret reality *imaginatively*, we cant have science, mathematics, technology without doing so - the capacity of the brain is greater than its confirmable contents, and must be.

Then what is the position of children - those who can be told stories, and those even younger who exist only on signs, messages floating to them in bottles over a dark ocean? How quickly children despair! - how quickly their world crumbles! They have no philosophy or theology - only a few signs. And yet their brain has its infinite capacity. If the primitive person counts only on three fingers - then his hands have fifty million fingers, the uncounted ones. Little of him is god, and much of him the devil - within his limited world he may be more godlike than say the European in his space-rocket (Levi-Strauss is certainly right about such things) - but the gods have to learn to do the devil's work - it's the only way in which human beings can be made. This means that the child will live strongly in its imagination: and that its first lessons will be an attempt to instil cause-and-effect into the imaginary. Why? - in order to humanise itself. In telling and believing fairy stories the child is trying to take responsibility for the world. If there are ogres, then the child must learn to live with them - if the giant cant be taught to cry he must be cut down. He cant be propitiated. That is why children are extremists. A businessman may concentrate on the Stock Exchange, a soldier may concentrate on the enemy: areas of his mind - which must be responded to - are occupied for him by external social powers. The child cant manage this, it can only question: it has all the responsibilities of Einstein and Newton and Plato - and it's that which makes the child a poet and artist, he must incorporate cause-and-effect into the imaginary: it has to have a reality as great as that of sticks and stones, otherwise the child will despair. In this way the child may humanise the little kingdom it has, and place much of the world in it - but it will be profoundly wrong about the world. When the child imagines it is trying to be an adult; when adults imagine, they are very often trying to be like children. That is the tragedy of art.

There is no other way of producing the human mind than this. It's the consequence of our biological development and the nature of objectivity and what an objective statement is. Although I think structuralism provides very useful aesthetic and dramatic tools I dont think it explains human behaviour because it does not see the mind as a diachronic structure. Imaginatively the child will have structured the whole of the world - just as a religious person sees every part of the world as either God's or the devil's: there isnt an area beyond the three fingers which can be filled with general knowledge. All knowledge will either relate to or be achieved by a mind which is imaginatively holistic. Curiously, the child sees the world in highly political terms - it's a matter of power, rules, obedience, rewards etc.; the child relates to these things before it has a grasp of social constitutionality. This probably creates our secondary needs. If hunger is a primary need and leads to a certain sort of learning; then a secondary need, here, is a need for a child to establish good relations within spheres of power - the child has a political need before it has political tools, expressions etc. This is why, it seems to me, the imagination is one of the most politicized of all parts of the mind - and why politics often uses its language. All political movements, of any depth, create their own aesthetics - and this is both an objective need (how to create new truths and distribute them) and also a subjective need, a subjectivity in change needing new supports and structures.

So of course I agree with you that our imagination has its origins and dynamics in the nature of human infancy and childhood. If humans were rigidly innately programmed for any society (not a biological possibility, of course) then there could be no history - since social practice couldnt change, there would be no need to respond to new technology organisationally and subjectively because new technology couldnt be created. This is only possible because human beings begin without knowledge and then socially learn - and a biological consequence is: the brain with a capacity larger than its contents (and therefore able to learn, and needing to appropriate infinity) placed in a society where its owner is physically incapable of full-knowledge and full-anticipation, must have its foundations in the imagination, and must achieve its psychological impulses and energies within the area in which the imagination relates to reality. A young person's early efforts at drawing with a pencil have imaginative, creative value - early efforts at using a knife or wiring an electric plug are merely inefficient: *but*, the imaginative is profoundly social and political.

I dont want to go too deeply into the psychology of children, but perhaps I could say that these secondary needs often become primary. The secondary needs imply some social experience and learning. Hunger is not a basic need because it has no meaning until it's comparable with repletion - a child may be taught what hunger is because it has previously been fed, for instance. But a secondary need has a further characteristic: it involves a structure in the imagination. This makes it stronger than a merely physical need, and not weaker as you might suppose. We run society in order to eat - but when necessary people will starve themselves to death for their causes, risk their lives, be celibate - climb mountains to test their self-image and so on. Really, we need only eat, copulate and shit - history and the vast world communities are created by secondary needs, they are the fruit of the imagination, and so are technology and science - as far as the existential human being is concerned. Is that an odd thing for a dialectical materialist to say? No - Im not saying that technology is an objective creation of the imaginary - the world is objectively real and structurally positive; and technology, once it incorporates various forms of energy (physical and formal) certainly applies pressure on society and subjectivity (that's why there is history); but human drives, energies, ambitions always exceed their needs, their physical primary needs - which is the reason why they will sometimes place secondary needs over primary needs. We will kill and die for our secondary needs and many people do

- far many more than die by fighting over a meal. Or a girl? Well does this mean sexual *instincts* are stronger? I find instinct a misused and more or less useless word. It seems that imagination, in a child, puts greater importance, very often, on personal and family relations than on primary needs such as those for food. The sexual "instinct" is more powerful simply because it's more imaginary, fused with greater imaginative experience and learning - created by that learning: since it reflects a greater segment of the child's horizon. I think I can sum up the child's secondary needs in one phrase: radical innocence.[3] A child is often made to feel guilty - and it may be that it can be so scared and depressed that it loses the existential conviction that it has a right to live. If that happens the child dies - or lives a living death - it stops functioning socially. Of course this state doesnt necessarily imply that it's the victim of bad parents - it may come about through a sequence of chance and illness etc.

What happens is that the mental world of the child, holistically formed, goes into the adult world, and is co-opted by the adult world of further learning and experience. The mind is already imaginatively articulate and energized - but not objectively informed. That is a great liability - since many adult activities will be seen as metaphors for the already existing mind: but if it werent so the human species would be static and without history. In a sense reality is always a metaphor for the imagination. Why should living and dying, beauty and ugliness, matter to us - if there's no god to put concerned souls into us? Because as children we took responsibility for the world - it's the only way we could bear to live in it. Cynicism and banal opportunism are adult diseases. This is all very stupid no doubt! - Im concerned about the world, I have an aesthetic and ethical preoccupation with it, because I was once a child - ? Then I'll forget that and just rip others off. But on Wall Street they say: America's a lovely country - and better dead than red. The political case is this: unless the workings of society can be understood objectively and rationally (and by now it must be clear that doesnt mean at the cost of the imagination - the cost of that is always madness) then objectivity leaks back dangerously into the imaginative and the imaginative is made real: and this means that the adult becomes like a child who's the victim of external, malignant powers (this is already a prominent theme in Western "art") - and so the imagination gains control of technology. Instead of technology being able to restructure a form of consciousness appropriate to itself, an earlier form of

---

[3] Bond defines "radical innocence" in "Commentary on *The War Plays*," *The War Plays* Methuen, London 1991. 251-8.

consciousness (with its imaginative apprehensions) directs technology (actually it did this through, in the past, the public appearance of the social ownership of technology; more and more, now, by the use of media - bits of imaginative-hardware floating in society - supporting imagination in a way that comes between it and reality, turning imagination into a fantasy which isolates it from its vital ability to learn and perceive) so that technology becomes (at least partly) the expression of irrationality and not the ground for increased rationality.

You see that the various components of the mind and experience constantly interact and reshape and qualitatively re-existentialize each other. We are changed because our external environment acts on us but it can only do this (outside catastrophe) because we act on it. It's as if we read a book and from time to time as we did so one of the sentences spoke to us and said: No, understand me this way - and often as a consequence of this all the following sentences in the book changed their contents. I think that human beings have art aesthetics as part of their secondary - and therefore more important - needs, and why these things are accompanied with struggle, with the acquiring of skill - and have been related to religious and political authorities and interpretations: they are the skin which binds the individual's mind to his social existence, really (to be metaphorical) to his society.

Bombs dont care how many people they destroy: if a bomb could speak it wouldnt boast to a grenade that it had destroyed Hiroshima. Caring about anything is an expression of radical innocence. That innocence appears within the guilt of Hitlerism, the selfishness of imperialism, the merchandising of weapons, in perverted forms - but that's what it is, and it forms the justification, and worse the justified impulse, for these things. So is humanity forever a morass? Hamlet and Lear and Oedipus were acting and struggling for radical innocence (so was Antigone, but the theatres were largely owned by men). Why is one corrupt and the other civilized and cultured? I think it's because the corrupt radical innocence speaks for the self, it's the imagination of the child controlling technology, let loose on society, it is *self*-language: the other I think is social language, it can only articulate the child's need for radical innocence, the impulse to accept responsibility for the world in which it is, by "speaking its society." No fascist is a universalist, there's always an irredeemably evil enemy: the radical innocence of Hamlet and Lear is universalist: it asks what is a human being and how should a human being live? Dostoevsky thought that if God was dead everything was possible. He had an argument with Grand Inquisitors but no political response to the real problems they raised. In fact if there is no God then part of the imagination - which had been wrongly occupied - can be restored to human responsibility. We become responsible for our world. Gods have never stood against evil, prevented it - we were told to submit. In fact, even if there were a God he could only appear in the human mind (note that he'd have to speak the language we'd learned in the experience that formed the mind) as a devil - though no doubt in a bland or alluring form; he would justify evil actions, make them necessary.

I think Hamlet's questions only have political answers. Class structures in society deform consciousness, they make the imagination rancid and dark or banal, trivial and self-pitying. I dont think human beings are innately good, have an innate need to love or hate one another. But I think that the curiously wounded condition into which human beings are born is their great strength: because it leads to the creation of secondary needs which become much more important than animal needs, and which can be summed up as existential, radical innocence. What becomes of this is a consequence of society. A culture obviously has a hegemonic teaching but it also provokes tensions and assurgent cultures within it. I think this is because new technologies make necessary new forms of behaviour (and therefore at the same time new exponential forms of consciousness) which conflict with the existing culture which is - necessarily - the guardian of the existing forms of social ownership and the way in which social organisation of technology is ordered. When these relations break down obviously the mental mass of society is in upheaval and conflict.

I can now return to the problem I started with. I suppose the imagination - and its existential emotional expressions - are in constant parturition. To re-use an emotion is to change it. There is no permanent emotional language. There is no emotional authentication of experience. Emotions may be lies, oratory or the truth. An emotion is not interesting: what is interesting is only the explicit idea it articulates. Emotions must always be treated as if they were a foreign language: we have no right to understand them without further explanation. The audience do not share the stage's emotions. We have to accept responsibility for the stage's emotions. And that's the difference between the stage and the street.

If I see a rape on the street I intervene - that's how I accept a social responsibility. If I see a rape on the stage I dont intervene. Then why - am I merely a "voyeur?" No, I accept responsibility by understanding. The cultural crime is when the stage - the writer, actor or director - short-circuits this process and says there is nothing to understand, there is merely human nature, the eternally given. The stage ought to increase the understanding of the imagination by putting it in greater control of objectivity, giving it greater moral authority. Otherwise you leave the theatre saying "hang the rapist," or "hate the uncultured working class," or "the object of society is to protect my property." You can always quite properly write plays which have immediate practical aims: saying things such as in a plague dont drink unboiled water. But societies are also articulations of secondary needs - and the use of these to suppress processes which form in the mind: and we have to find a way of expressing this.

In classical Athens the stage was owned by the rulers of the community. On the stage they openly put their society up for trial, allowed it to be examined, and then fused their audience with society in such a way that it enabled the audience to an extent at least to express its radically-innocent need to be human: what you were purged of was not fear but doubt; certainly much doubt was left, but this would be glamourised by being submitted to the gods of fate. But theatre is a dangerous medium because it must always be founded on some truth - such truth that has to be admitted before an audience will accept the ideological redirection: Euripides traded on the admitted truths so that they began to deglamourize the gods - and so the theatre was brought to its end: if the gods lost their glamour the audience began to look silly. Yet the audience knew they were not: they were the bearers of radical innocence. So they must change the society in which the theatre was built. But the technological apparatuses for a changed society were not there (steam was used to work stage machinery, slaves were used to work the mines and serfs the fields).

Shakespeare is as obsessed with the supernatural as any witch-hunting bigot. Yet he uses it differently. Hamlet is afraid of dying - not particularly smitten with living. Shakespeare sees that his society is changing. He articulates new forms of consciousness, restructures the working of the subjective being, becomes his own consciousness. Hamlet is a great speaker; when he dies they say: The rest is silence. By making Hamlet a politician Shakespeare speaks his audience's new political responsibilities. In the history plays people fight for the throne - they dont doubt their moral or political worth - if they do, they say I dont want it. Hamlet says: Should I? Not, can I? Before god said who was to be king. So politically Hamlet is an advance and within the political limitations of the new bourgeois society - he teaches political openness. But only within limits: the imagination puts the ghosts, witches, devils *out* there - just as James the Ist did -

and even the Diggers did. Soon the progressive forces will shut the theatres - because Hamlet questions when ghosts still speak.

We can respond to these earlier theatres because of the disciplines by which they ask questions. We dont accept their political answers, although these were vital to the original audiences - and indeed, the reason why the plays were written. We accept their "artistic experiences" - as abstractions, as eternal truths. But take away the blank verse and Hamlet doesnt exist. Who says truth must be written in blank verse, that blank verse makes truth eternal? Take away the blank verse and Hamlet's questions exist. We can, as it were, get so much from Hamlet only because it is irrelevant, the play matters because it's lost its meaning: so we can respond to a human being at full stretch who will not accept self-deceit: an existential authenticity - Claudius kills both Hamlet and his father because Claudius is corrupt - Hamlet dies for his radical innocence: within the political limitations of his time he cant do more. When Brecht and Jules Laforgue poke fun at Hamlet they misunderstood his strength - Hamlet commanded many divisions into battle. Hamlet has the caution of the gun-fighter. Psychologically Hamlet is killed by a pistol shot, and to the sound of gun fire: the sword and the bomb on stage together.

So where does this put us? It means that we "shouldnt play the character." Not at any rate as that's normally understood - and here I think I disagree with you. Of course Im asking for the impossible - but when we set out to discover the Indies we might hopefully discover America? I know what method actors mean when they talk about discovering the character. I do it when I write. My characters have a character-unity, and as I write they speak for themselves, they have their own vivacity, I dont plan what they're going to say next anymore than when I begin to write "character" I am conscious of the "er" as I write the "ch." And if I make a character say something it wouldnt the character more or less tells me not to (rarely happens: we seem to understand each other). (That is a half-truth). And, I usually begin a play from something physical - I dont know what a character's saying, cant feel it, unless I know what they've got in their hands, I feel them moving their heads as they speak (as I write), and what I write is improvised. I admit all that. And yet I have to say: dont play the character? But didnt I write a character? Well, what ever we do, now, is an adjustment: actors are still going to have legs and voices, if we abolish the scenery (usually a good idea) at least they have to come on stage, or appear (or be heard) under it - there will be masses of continuity. But suppose Reagan appearing on TV suddenly picked his nose - a small change from the normal? But surely significant. And in fact not a joke. He has cancer of the nose. Perhaps it was a scratch at a cancerous discomfort? The joke would suddenly become very serious. So was it a joke - or a drama? A piece of senility - or a dramatic appeal for sympathy? The gesture means nothing outside its context. The emotion means nothing outside its context. The character means nothing outside its context.

Is this alienation? Alienation isnt a static device. Were comic sword fights in the bloodbaths of the Coliseum alienation? Apparently they were degradations - a way perhaps of allowing the real deaths to carthesize the audience but at the same time (by such ludicrousnesses) filling them with guilt and self-triviality. Are the comic (and cruel) carpenters in the *Mystery* plays alienations? They seem more like subversions on the part of the audience against the authorities. Let's settle (for the sake of argument) on the idea that an alienation is a comment on what is shown - at the very least divorcing it from its usual interpretation or response. Traditional societies are ones in which practice and theory are closely annealed, one almost disappearing into the other. I can give the example of the wooden plough. It's made by the same carpenter who makes the cradles and coffins and church pews. Its skills are mainly learned through repetition. The object is soaked with its own meaning. Kneeling in the church, bending at the plough, are postures soaked with their own meaning. Does the prayer ask god to put up the price of pigs? Is this prayer alienated? But if you look closely at the tear, sweat and hunger marks on the mans face - no. What are the users instructions on a hi-fi set? They come printed and probably are marked with a foreign origin - the translation into the user's language (of this ultra modern piece of equipment) might even be bad. Someone prays to god to look after their shares on Wall Street? Look at the face? - fat, but with all the anxieties of hunger, surfeited but with all the desperateness of greed? That, at last would be an alienation. But suppose it's some lonely widow in a small town praying for the same thing - those frail hands must presumably be patted by a Wall Street pirate if she's to be comforted? Is that alienation?

In a sense many more activities are now more naturally alienated than they were before because more and more things come with instructions - interpretations of performance in order to achieve success. Things become divorced from their theories when the theories need to be written down. (It's like the Pope having to come out of the Vatican. The first time he kissed the tarmac we blinked and wondered if this offended Christ? Now we wonder if he has shares in the tarmac company.) In a sense TV and always-available radio alienate all experience. Alienation for me means giving something a meaning. Brecht perhaps needed to divorce things from very traditional meanings. But dont we live in an often meaningless society - where things are given spurious urgencies and vitalities by invoking fear or envy? We need to identify new meanings and then describe them. At the moment the user's instructions on a room full of objects have got mixed up - people are foolishly turning knobs that arent there, looking at screens showing images upside down, hitting with a hammer something they should be brushing with oil and so on. So there is social chaos and violence. Drama seems to be whatever adds to it - or makes it bland. But Im not now going to say that we should get the right instructions onto the right gadgets - because it's a case of having to create new things, new understandings.

I can only approach it in this way. The actor must play the play and not the character. So he must define the role his character has in the play. We assume that everyone in the same room is in the same world. This isnt so: a character may be in the same room as another but in a different world. As we have at all costs to avoid the surreal, which is now just escapism, we have to be careful that they *are* in the same room: they are sitting at a table drinking tea (drawing room scene). But what are the worlds - by that I mean, how are they creating their world at that moment? How will it be different afterwards - think of it as concretely as you would building a wall. Look, why does the brick that man has just put in the wall have blood on it? Because for him its an execution wall? And why does that man put in his brick upside down? Because he will be shot on the wall and that is how he will fall? So is the tea table the floor of a slaughter house? Look at the man's hands, are they a butcher's hands? How do you know - because they are very clean? How does a butcher wipe his hands on his apron in the presence of a lady? - dont ladies normally (even now!) wear aprons? Now perhaps we know how a butcher will handle his teacup at the table - it's the ways he wipes the blood off his hands onto the apron? But he isnt a butcher, he is Brian having tea with a lady? No, that's merely his room: his world is the abattoir - only dont show it. But he's come to give the lady something - he's bringing gifts and wants nothing in return - except that she believes he isnt a butcher. Oh my god she's serving ham sandwiches. Now this is all just a visit of condolence, and we could play grief and commiseration. But actors should never forgive their characters - even when they're innocent - if the "world" situation isnt being told. I mean by that phrase, the truth of the total situation. When it is, the character (as written) will probably recognise its own strength - or at least insistency - and that will be played. When the situation is understood then the character can be played, but not the other way round - as Hamlet (and his author) thought. This means (as an example) that in the penultimate scene of my play *Summer* some of the characters are in a farce and must play it as such, with farce timing and movement etc., and others are in a tragedy (I dont flinch at the word) and must play it as such. When I told the actress playing the farce character to play it as a farce she said, "Oh well, if you want to spoil your beautiful scene."[4] Yet when this character is played as farce the scene is alive, taut and demanding - when it isnt it's noble, lachrymose and maudlin. I suppose Claudius is pretty farcical, when Gertrude drinks the poison from the cup? (The gun sound? Hamlet is killed to the sound of gun fire). But for us such distinctions have a much greater meaning: because we live in a world of disassociated instructions, of electric light and not the seasons, of machine sounds and not natural sounds.

If I say dont play the character it's because the character isnt enough like the character to be interesting. You have to go to extremes. The same woman character in *Summer* at one time says she's dead: then play her as a zombie in that scene, as near to a corpse as you can. In that scene she's spat on. How does a corpse react when its spat upon. Well, the "society lady" she is would be very upset. But a corpse? Well a corpse isnt upset by anything. Dont you believe it. Find out what the corpse is upset by and then you'll understand the whole of her life. Suppose you bury a corpse in a tie it didnt like. Why should I do that? Well the corpse is your husband and you hated him. (I see). So what does the corpse do? He spends all his time trying to get it off? No corpses cant move. Well he spends all his time trying to get someone else to take it off. Or, would he spend all his time working out what he's going to tell god when judgement day comes: Look god you see what sort of woman she was, no wonder I got cross... Well you said Im dead not my husband. Yes but now we know why she likes good clothes and how she looks at them when she's got them on - will they look good for eternity? Even when she's wearing her wedding dress? Especially then, it'll help the audience: it's a shroud.

What Im trying to do is this: we depend totally on realism - I dont like the surreal or the fantastical -but we need to relate it to the imaginary: because our

---

[4] Bond refers to the National Theatre production of *Summer* which opened in the Cottesloe on 27 January, 1982.

lives are to an extent metaphors which take on the reality of facts. Now if I create a metaphor, say: "The snow is writing its memoirs." I then say to the actor, play that. The actor has to make a permanent record -yet at the same time we are reminded of the transitoriness of things, and the vanity of much ambition. Then if the snow melts: what is left - what first begins to appear through the snow? Well I probably wouldnt know what that is. But you must try to write it. It's difficult? Yet you will write: I was born on - . Perhaps then you should just cry and walk out of the room? That's writing memoirs?! For the time being. But the text says he sits and writes. Well write as if he'd just cried and walked out of the room. And then we begin to get a system: because the actor will usually want to act an actor - and an actor picks up a piece of paper in a certain way. But you can also pick up a piece of paper and show why Caesar was assassinated (think of the various uses of paper and writers in Shakespeare's *Julius Caesar* - you cant act his documents till you know what Shakespeare was angling for with them). Finding the character is the easiest part of playing - the character is the easiest part of playing - the character merely moves in and takes over when the real work is done. The character is to the role what stitches are to the garment. Dont let the character capture the role - fight the character off as long as you can. The character is always the last stage. Build a prison, commit a crime, build a court, hold a trial, pass a sentence, lock the convict up in his cell - and one day you will meet the convict on the street: he will have escaped - because there is a radical-innocence. Perhaps the character will be walking well or in a terribly contorted way (in this matter all assaults are committed on the self). Take the character apart, act the extremes, and so avoid the stereotypes and the tricks by which crudities are disguised as subtleties. You can act these if you wish - they'll have a certain reward for you and the audience. But you wont have got to the fertile ground where the imagination asks questions - you will merely be responding to received answers. There is an important point here because I think that at basis characters are paradoxes, and you cant act a paradox - you can only act the consequence of being a paradox. No good characters makes much sense. Hamlet didnt notice his opponent's sword was unguarded. It's lesson number one. Any private soldier checks if his rifle's loaded when he takes it from the rack - and by now Hamlet is noticing everything - and even staring at the sword point! So you must act what it is makes him not notice - that's how to act the fight. To miss something really important you must put it under your nose (as Poe knew). So the fight will have lots of pauses with sudden lethal attacks each time he might notice? Obviously we must approach the sword fight by considering how someone looks down a microscope and misses what's there: why is the truth seeker avoiding the truth? Yes, you can ask how well trained Hamlet is and how overweight (and other social realistic questions) and act that - but you must act the naked sword and why the whole court doesnt see it? Ah perhaps they're not very interested in this boring squabble? But if it happened in the White House - everyone would look? Perhaps the equivalent would be two senators stabbing each other in the back - must happen all the time. Perhaps it's a sordid little scuffle in the corner of some world? Yes perhaps it's a great fight in the room - but in its world it's a sordid little squabble. So there are two points. You should be true to a text. Most modern updatings of Jacobean texts, for example, dont seem to move the plays into our times but push them back into their own times by creating an incomprehensible layer of artificiality. You gain nothing by altering the text unless it's purely for the sake of clarity - removing incomprehensibly long references and so on. It's better to *use* the play's problems by finding directorial and acting uses for them. Really the text is ever only offering you a series of problems and the more carefully constructed these problems are the better the play. The problems arent riddles with snap answers (once found) but opportunities for deployments. The other point is this. The play doesnt provide its meaning: the meaning *is* the performance, the way the problems are solved - not discovering the way the play seems to insist they're solved. This of course can encourage the arbitrary and artificial. So you have to come down to basics. A play in the end tells the actors, director and audience what they are - at least in relation to the play. It exists through their choices - not through secret discoveries of the self which mysteriously reveal meaning. So it depends on the interpreters' (in the first place) understanding of the meaning of their own lives - how else could they portray the characters? That means a philosophy of society - consciously or not. An actor commits a vow to the audience that he will tell the truth. The actor likes to be on speaking terms with the audience. But remember, audiences respond well to uncomfortable truths - provided they think you have earned the right to tell them. Of course some people run away from the truth. This is not a reason to encourage them with lies. It's up to you to choose, if you're working in theatre, whether you want to waste your life or not.

The philosophy you have will determine the direction of the decisions you make about your character - and there's no way in which this can be otherwise. So important theatre comes down always to this: do you have a philosophy which enables you, within the historical limits of your time, to express your humanity? To do that you have to meet certain conditions - not of behaviour but of understanding. Your society will be the depository of certain information and technology which will be changing behaviour in your society. You will observe this change, you cant avoid it; unless you take into consideration the information, and the practice, which have caused this change - you cant interpret it, and it cant become part of you. Instead you will react to it, exploit it, concede to its dangerous state of control - and contribute to our present danger. There seems to be a spate of American plays about Einstein. This isnt a good sign - it's a pushing away of knowledge into exotic figures, instead of bringing home its consequences on the streets and in the houses of our cities and villages. There are no aesthetic ways of avoiding this responsibility.

It's difficult to write about things one really needs to show. But I think that out of the sort of practice I've been describing new aesthetic methods could be produced. The risk is that almost anything can be made to work on the stage: what happens is usually a mixture of Freudian reductionism and sociobiological behaviourism - a reduction to a common human nature, which we can respond to warmly - or regret and punish. Very often precisely those things which the Greeks found tragic we should laugh at; and what they found funny, we should grieve at. This is because we have different powers at hand. Democracy may easily become very impotent. All the time it must be stimulated by the politico-psyches of its members. This means that art is still, as it has always been, at the foundations of our social life: if the imagination becomes moribund or fantastical, then reality becomes dangerous, impotently hyperactive and dies.

The philosophy has to be politically broad. But the aesthetics of the stage probably best begin in small things - small questions like "why did no one notice the unguarded sword? - in a play of questions and examinations." You cant put the epic content out to the director's schemes or the mise en scene. It has to go into the foundations of the acting - to find that the basis of the acting isnt a response but a question or questions. I think that people on the street are actively producing themselves in this way - and that acting is valuable in that it can take this a stage further. You cant resort to a "this is so" or "that works" or "people are like that" or "I've found it." That's putting people into rooms and you must put rooms into worlds, as I've tried to explain. In *The Sea* is Mrs. Rafi's long speech self-pity? Or is it knowledge on which she cant act? Should we pity her as she pities herself? Or is her pity really a judgement on the audience? The funeral

was comic. Perhaps she's now at the audience's funeral? So should there be a
severity about her judgement. A dignity? Or better, a hollowness which will
help the audience most? That is the most important of the questions. The most
important work in the theatre is always the work of the audience. Dont consider
this a cliche - it's an important truth. What work are we requiring of the audience
at this moment? - and you cant avoid that rather dictatorial responsibility Im
afraid. You cant take away their freedom, but you can demand that they exercise
it - not doze or be lulled. So how do you do the speech? The author alas gives us
no guidance. And nor does the character - because each of the other characters in
the play would see and hear her differently. Are we to assume that the audience
are in a privileged character and see her objectively? But if we've been talking
about characters as if they were concrete things to be discovered, then this must
also be true of the audience and so their way of seeing her is predetermined: you
have no choice, except to avoid the problem by being arbitrary? The audience
arent in the stage of the actor at early rehearsals, saying "who on earth am I (the
character)... ?" because the audience bring their character with them. But you
dont all meet on day one. The actors will have worked and discovered - and so
the audience is being presented with a different role to play. The actor (on day
one) says: how do I load the gun? The audience are having the gun pointed at
them. So their own normal character is suspended - and likely to rebound all the
more dogmatically sometimes. So the audience will be learning how to respond
to the speech - not bringing a determined, characterological interpretation: unless
they react. And so they will be doing work not unsimilar to the actor's: they will
be discovering themselves. And so the speech becomes very strange: in one way
it's like someone with no words talking to others with no ears. The audience is
addressed, but overhears (even when directly addressed). The actress speaks but
is interpreted by her character. This means that there is great freedom of choice -
and the actress must find her particular truth, her particular way of telling it. But
then really she is telling it to her character: and the truth of the acting is nearer to
that - the actor plays his role in front of the character, says, "that is how I see
you:" the actor speaks the lines to his character, and *then* he enters into serious
dialogue with the audience and doesnt merely collude with them. The character
belongs to the audience and must not be lied about. But the audience are many -
and some corrupt. So the actor must rely on his radical innocence, which is his
primary/almost-primal ability to judge and assess. And I think that's what *you*
mean when you talk about the character being inside you: I say *no*, because that

primary necessity will have taken vital cognisance of all the individual's
subsequent experience and will only be able to satisfy (to the extent it can) itself
by judging and understanding the events and elements of that experience: you
have identified a need, rampant in the artist and alive in everyone, but not how it
is to be fulfilled.   An "instinct" has no meaning without learning: till then it's
merely a reflex, and its owner would observe the consequences not experience the
need.   Emotions teach the intellectuation of cause-and-effect, make that a
grounding for mental consciousness: therefore emotions are questions. Of course
there are physical satisfactions - enjoyment, letting off steam etc - and we can
observe and understand them, and respond to them - but the moment anything of
consequence happens, the moment it involves our imagination - then there are
questions, and these originate in radical-innocence. And so the actor must ask
these questions: there's nothing waiting there to be discovered, things must be put
together. When this is done, then it's as if the actor were free to consent - his
radical-innocence authenticates the work and it becomes actable - and
performable within the rhythms and pacing of the stage. But the *process* must be
understood and protected. After all, the inadequate artist feels as authentic as the
good one. The actor can always blind the audience, collude with them. This
happens through a process of reductionism - and I take that to be a fact of
experience, learnable in the theatre. There *is* a different aesthetic experience.
And this happens not when the audience is told what it knows, but asked
questions in ways that are encouraging but stringent.

I try to establish a scheme for theatre practice based on an understanding
of the way the mind works, knows, experiences and creates anything. Theatre is
concerned in a special way with the functioning of consciousness. The spectator
observes images which happen to be real and beyond his volitional control, but
which nevertheless have obvious similarities to the imagery of his own
imagination. The theatre worker has to use his imagination to create these images
and spectacles for audiences. So it seems that theatre work must be based on an
analytical understanding of the mind's working before it can be about anything
else: otherwise it merely becomes the initiator of a series of mirrors, each
reflecting into the other. But the mind is all frontier (although some of it's
submerged that doesnt change the working-situation: the boundary between
America and Canada reaches down to the earth's centre). A frontier seems a
boundary   without   content: it   is   only   activated   in   relation   to
time/objects/events/organisation in the real world. But because it is a frontier it is

the process by which reality may be apprehended and at the same time created; to use an image, you cant make a distinction here between the wrappings of a parcel and the hands that carry the parcel. The mind is objectively dealing with itself and the world in a special way. To continue with the parcel image, we carry the parcel only at certain points, sometimes adjusting the load, and learning (like specialized porters) increasingly more efficient ways of carrying the burden. It seems that human beings have no way of understanding what's in the parcel: that's Wittgenstein's barrier - but we have no *need* to know it. We can learn to carry the burden in such a way that it becomes less primitively crushing - though perhaps more demanding? - and here the use of the image runs out. The important point is that imagination isnt arbitrary - though it can be made, ideologized, into the frivolous, manic etc. We can talk, in the theatre, of human activity under two aspects: the real and the imaginary. If I put on my boots that is a real activity. But it involves the imagined in various ways. If the boots are military I take on the ethos of the military. If they're farmer's boots I take on the mystique and legends of soil and land. If they're factory worker's boots - then I take on the conflict of cities, industrial relations, urban culture, hypermarkets etc. Each object becomes a reference point for the world in which it is. These points arent static, they move in statistics, stories, trials etc. I couldnt put on the boots unless they belonged to such systems - and unless I imagined them. The systems have their own reality but they affect me only because they also invoke and require that I imagine them. If the army boots I put on are spotless, is that an image of military efficiency or of Pilate washing his hands? It must be one or the other - or some other third - or the audience will provide one: you and the action should decide what it is, and therefore the actor should decide how the laces need to be tied by him. The imagined is the interpretation of what is happening -and on the stage this is what is concrete, even more than the raw event. What tends to happen in method acting, directing and writing, is that the imagination is impoverished and usually appears as the deviant, anti-social or neurotic. This means that the real (street) imagination has become reified in dogmatic, sterile ways; it represents orthodoxy and its licensed permissiveness, and any social questioning which requires a solution (rather than an answer: sweets for cut knees) is seen and dramatized (the examples are very many) as deviant or insane. Yet no society can support itself without radically questioning itself. Imagination is the faculty in which the vital secondary needs, about which I wrote, have their reality: an objective relation to the objective world, yet always an historical "reading" of objectivity as it co-functions with subjective consciousness.

The function of art is to bring reality to the imagination, to use it to reinterpret and so change the objective, social world, from which it achieves the impulse to change - as it were, it's the way in which reality suggests (and sometimes demands) that the individual change it. What usually happens in the theatre is that imagination is symbolized as icons or evasive abstractions (Churches prefer stone and wood idols; when they make banners they like them to be of thick material the wind cant blur - static) or seen as a source of regressive pleasure: as if even the infant's pleasures werent caught up in power relations.

I think theatre must work in this way: Firstly it must identify its characters' "rooms" - the events and objects in terms of social realism: what does this character earn, how many people travel on this train, where did the bishop go to school, which companies own this town and who owns the companies etc. These are factual matters, and unless you want to say that art is entirely involved in the mystical, abstract, aesthetically pure etc, then presumably you wouldnt quarrel with this. Then there's the next stage, the one that's neglected or misunderstood. The misunderstanding makes us as useless as savages who take bullets out of a gun and throw them by hand at their enemy: we have to treat the imagined as realism. We have to reverse what is normally done, in order to get to the root political nature of events and objects, and to create an interaction between stage-imagined, street-imagined, audience-imagined and actor-imagined. We shouldnt treat the imagination as exotic, something extra, vague, mental: the imagination is concrete, determined-and-consequential, objective. Often this means treating the metaphor literally, since metaphor is one of the most characteristic forms of the imagined. This means that imagination cant be allowed to follow its own structural impulses (though they're probably there) but that the imaginative story is the proof of the facts - and it must have its own contents. The realistic function concerns acts such as putting on boots and getting run over by automobiles: the imaginative function is "if only you could see what you are doing now." See the murder from the point of view of the victim - and the dagger. You cant reach imaginative-realism by self-introspection. That will merely reduce awareness and recognition to subjective resources already determined and characterised, though they retain a viability (and rejuvenating potential as what I've described as radical innocence) - we have to see that these resources are the foundations of our lives, both in external movements in society and in internal movements in our consciousness. They are not static but in change, and so the imagination is like an energy saying: tell me a story to explain the facts. The social realism of imagination has enormous potential: it brings with it the whole range of experiences which are sometimes wrongly coded as tragic and comic, and its the foundation of any art that can sustain itself beyond its ability to immediately viscerally impress.

Theatre work means identifying social reality in its most mundane circumstances, and then bringing strict social realism to the imagined foundation of our experience. Putting on the boots, loading the gun or laying the table, cleaning a window and paying taxes for H bombs - all these events occur in imagination as much as in mundane reality. Sometimes the imagined is pushed out of consciousness but then so is the factual recording of what we're doing.

Imagination is the way in which objectivity uses us to make us part of it. A rope pulls a barge only when it's taut, when reality catches up on it. Imagination can be thought of as a rope that will pull barges even when it's slack - sometimes then it pulls barges faster; from time to time reality tightens its grip and then the imagined may become its most wayward and bizarre, till it floods out into reality and creates its own images in real flesh and real bricks: the wounds and ruins of war. The job of theatres is to make imagination taut by expressing it as social realism. There arent any further rules; talent and insight are of course needed. We have to use imagination objectively and morally, as the great teaching ability of our species which it is: to show reason in the mundane; to make imagination prove facts. We are more rational than other animals because we have imagination. On the other hand, it's our greatest danger - but if you're drowning you dont reject the rope merely because it's thrown to you by the hangman. Most political dramatists are afraid of the imagination, but it seems to me to be the bedrock of good political theatre. And if we dont use our imagination in this way, then we destroy the talents of the audience instead of nurturing them - and we cant do worse than that.

The boundary between objective analysis and intuition must be clearly worked out, and the objective analysis must be accurate. Given that, imagination will work (very often) in leaps. Does the rightness of a mathematical formula come into existence only when the last digit is in place, or is it being built up as it's being written down or composed in the head? - as a pile of bricks is built up into a wall? Clearly you cant talk in that way: but for the imagined insight to be correct the philosophy and analysis must be true - and then, and only then, can the imagination leap - laugh, cry, dance or whatever it is. The oddity of the imagination is that it shares characteristics of the physical and the abstract: both concrete and both corrigible. The imagination leaps when it has its feet firmly on the ground. I dont want to abolish intuitive insight etc - I cant imagine what doing that means. But I want to found it on the rational and the concrete - and I think we can do that.

Convention and social-discipline will impose one imagined interpretation on what you do. But you and the actor must choose your own imagined interpretation and the actor must act that, the designer objectify it etc. Sometimes changing society imposes its new imaginative ambience: consider Buchner's use of blades and blood so soon after the French Revolution - these images become conretisations of theories and events. Sometimes the play will help you: sometimes you will need to help the play. The play will have its own rhythms and its own structures - conversations will have shapes, turning points etc. You need to be nearly always true to these - but they wont conflict with what Ive called image-social-realism. And judgement is always need - I repeated this because it's so important. Remember Brecht's white faces for soldiers - method acting, TV acting, would probably use gore (I know Im being unfair about the method, sometimes sheer good sense overcomes the pitiful theory). Surely the soldiers' *victims* should be white with fear... but who has to be included among the victims? And I think we should always anchor what we do in realism - because surrealism, dada etc have now served their useful purpose and reality is now saturated with giantism, the viciously small, the absurd, the obscene. It means putting the extreme in such a way that the audience can now see that's what it is *yet at the same time it passes for normal.* Otherwise we've done nothing.

I began this letter intending to make only a few remarks over a sheet or two. But it got longer as I tried to fabricate a conversation with you. It appears to be in part a treatise! - and this is very irresponsible of it. Some of the examples occurred to me as a means of light-relief, to encourage you to continue with it. Yet the basis of what I want to say is serious. I have of course raised more questions than given answers.

To see the murder from the dagger's point of view. Macbeth's dagger floats in the air; then he produces a real one. Suppose he'd produced the real one first and then let it lead him? Buchner shows the dagger being bought. A surrealist film could show gold dollars being spattered from the gun. Make the gun jam - so that the murderer must use his hands, a bottle, a chair - a dagger?

And the gun slithers away over the concrete: those boring TV shoot outs! Or use the gun as a truncheon? As the gunman shoots a bullet goes into the huge mirror behind the victim: it's "shatter glass" so that it immediately turns into a white non-reflecting sheet covered with minute crazing - extend the victim's death against the white sheet you've now created (not too long) - as he falls bits of glass fall down onto him like snow: cut to the killer's hand having the money placed in it? - a bit baroque! So I refer you to the gun-lessons in *Human Cannon*. Remember, we die of solutions not problems: the point of theatre is to make the problem real.

Yours sincerely,

Edward Bond

SOME USEFUL SLOGANS
- Social realism of the facts - melodrama of the analysis
- Tendentious selection of the facts - social realism of the analysis
- The simpler the facts, the more extreme the interpretation - the more extreme the interpretation, the simpler (usually) the presentation
- We don't want facts to speak for themselves, we want them to listen
- Those who dance on graves call what they do performance arts
- When the method actor plays what he calls the "character" he is playing the puppet - in "systems acting" the actor points to the strings

Mark Ellis
London, W9   8 November 1988

Dear Mark Ellis,

Thanks for your letter. Im not sure whether we're not at cross purposes! My letter wasnt in any way meant to discourage you. To say nothing else: faced with the poverty of our present theatre, any experiment short of actual bloodshed must be good.

Much of what Artaud concerned himself with has been taken over - in impoverished and vicious forms - by some sorts of pop music and by the regular streams of TV adverts. But these usually attach to Artaud's abstract goals (which were to be made concrete by the audience accepting responsibility for what they saw) definite purposes - to sell something, or to put the audience in a state of excitement which has no practical outlet and so is equivalent to a state of being comatose. It seems to me that what you should now be able to do is understand more fully the social world into which your performances go. I think that often Artaud was reacting to the prisons and institutions in which he lived. The protest is important. But we need to understand how we build the institutions and prisons ourselves. It is a commonplace that creation has often entailed suffering. We need to ask where and in what way cruelty becomes creation: or does the act of creation lead to the audience's experience of your creation as *prior* to it? You have to ask always - in theatre - what is the work of the audience? Aristotle had a theory of cruelty in the theatre: he said it led to the purging of the audience so that they could be fitted more securely into their existing society. These cruelties of Greek theatre are less abstract than those of Artaud. But behind Artaud there are very definite problems. The Cenci derives from a Greek model - and not by accident.

I think that all the abstract images of Artaud in fact have actual counterparts in real life - yes all of them! And so the placing of these images in theatre doesnt win access to a world behind reality which in some way directs reality. The unconscious takes its imagery from social realism - it's just that we hide most of society's crises away. If you accept this about imagery - and theatrical effect - then you can see that the imaginary has a materialist basis - that really the dream is solid and has a social and psychological context.

What this means in terms of what you do on stage is a further question.

What the true dynamics of imagery are? How energy gets its objects? Theory cant solve aesthetic problems - but it can make the problems practical and provocative. Theory isnt so much the answer as the setting of the right problems. If theory replaces performance... well it's just bad theory.

I hope I havent discouraged you or seemed at odds with your theatre. I dont think I am. And I certainly didnt want to dissuade you from working on *Narrow Road*.

Yours sincerely,

Edward Bond

Nigel Jamieson
International Workshop Festival
London   10 January 1989

Dear Mr. Jamieson,

    Thanks for your letter and the kind remarks about my plays.

    I feel in something of a quandary. Im not sure what you mean by my achievements. I seem to have little contact with the professional theatre. My plays work better when they're done by amateur actors, I think. This is because instead of being in advance of social life - presenting aspects of the future on the stage and the solution of present troubles and problems in a theatricalising that makes things both more distant and objective yet more immediate and manageable - the stage seems to have retreated from it. It is merely entertainment - or gives an illusion of intellectual sophistication. The roles of street and theatre have been reversed - and perhaps this is a definition of reaction? Normally when street and theatre reverse their roles it is a time of some sort of revolution: and the revolution we're living in is reactionary. Now it is as if the street understood more about theatre than the stage. Going to the theatre now is usually a curious mixture of paying respect to the dead - like seeing a corpse - and getting a "fix" to prove you're alive. I feel our present theatre debases the human image and trivializes the human mind - or (worse) in the "serious" theatre barbarizes it.

    We dont understand what our society could use theatre for. Theatre is the most ancient of all the arts - yet each society has a specific use for it. Method acting is based on a 19th century concept of human behaviour and character. Left wing theatre wants to avoid the psyche - or see it in society, instead of society in it - which is the deeper fact. And so we get silence - the art of the significant pause - or frenzy: performance arts. And if acting has no meaning life cannot have meaning.

    I didnt mean to say that when I started this letter. I meant to write a simple acknowledgement. But it seems appropriate to let you know what I think about present theatre.

    I would like a theatre of my own. Of course I would then curse the burden of it! But it would make it possible for me to look at these problems in a disciplined and creative way. The present RSC production of *Restoration* makes me sad.[1] I enjoyed the play - but how superficial the acting is, even when its good! (I cant avoid the paradox: good actors can be a pleasure even when what they're doing is going only half the journey!) - and whenever the play tries to create dramatic structures appropriate to our needs, then the production is lost.

Actors and directors always need to ask not "What is it?" and "How do I make it work?" (anyone can make anything *work*!) but "What shall I use it for?" That means what is the supporting philosophy. The action will not then be a demonstration of that philosophy - a lesson. It will be instances of that philosophy in action, the play will not illuminate the philosophy, but the other way round. All modern philosophy - Marx, Wittgenstein, the deconstructionists, even Freud (though he can be captured by the Method and sociobiology) - make that necessary - because that is what modern personality has become: and that is what the street needs of the theatre. You could say that all incidents in a play are reducible to someone applying for a job and being unable to supply any character references. I try to portray the development of life - the National, the RSC, and the Court are interested only in making a killing.

Yours sincerely,

Edward Bond

---

[1] *Restoration* was staged by the Royal Shakespeare Company at the Swan Theatre, Stratford-upon-Avon, 13 September, 1988.

Oleg Yefremov
International Stanislavsky Centre
Moscow   13 February 1989

Dear Mr. Yefremov,

Thank you for inviting me to the recent Stanislavsky conference. It was not possible for me to attend.

Stanislavsky's work remains important. But his "method" has been largely misunderstood and used to support philosophies and attitudes he would have found unacceptable. In America the "method" has degenerated into the "treatment" - a way of injecting false life into morbid and sterile artistic philosophies. How we see the actor - and understand his or her creative process - is always dependent on how we see and understand the psychological and social life of the audience. If the actor gets his work wrong he corrupts the audience by giving them a false image of themselves. Art creates human nature in relation to our social and economic lives - it does not seek out primeval sources of value within us. When the actor creates a role he has to find the other characters within the character he is playing: value lies in the arbitration and judgement between these characters. In the same way the director needs not to create one world on the stage - but to show the many worlds there always are in one place, the many worlds there are in one room: this is how we proceed from past history, to present history, to future history: really art may be understood as the history of the future.

Yours sincerely,

Edward Bond

Calum MacCrimmon
Worcester College of Higher Education
Henwick Grove, Worcester   6 March 1989

Dear Calum MacCrimmon,

Thanks for your letter. I'll try to answer some of your further questions.

About violence in my plays: why? I grew up in a world war. I remember very well the day it ended. A sense of relief. After all a lot of skilled people had devoted a lot of energy for many nights in a row trying to kill me. I thought the world would be different. Of course I was young and couldnt see very far. Violence returned very quickly. Indeed peace in Europe inaugurated the period of even greater violence: the colossal threat of nuclear weapons. When states defend themselves by such immoral and grotesque means, violence seeps into the rest of society - into every part of it. Seeps or pours torrentially. Otherwise it would be as if the air were filled with rain that stopped a few inches from the ground. If governments threaten each other with force then people will read force into their society and their own lives. They will find a way of living in resorting to violence - and a meaning, excuse, explanation for their lives in it. (We are animals and so...etc.) This pervasive sense of violence corrupted art. The corruption took the form of the Absurd. It probably derived technically partly from surrealism and Dadaism - but it is very different. Those earlier art forms concerned themselves with an idealised world of art - an almost Platonic other world: in which beauty was found in the nonmechanical, the impractical. By its otherworldly beauty it was meant to be a criticism of ordinary bourgeois, commercial, exploited life. It as it were floats over that life. But the philosophy of the Absurd claimed to be a statement about foundations. It was meant to show that life was meaningless. That beauty and ugliness were the same. That attempts to remove human suffering merely produced more suffering. That our condition was hopeless. It claimed to be a moral statement about foundations. It took political violence and separated it from any judgement. But if you live in a society where a banknote has a meaning - an exchangeable value - then everything else has a meaning: but unfortunately the meaning is derived from money. The philosophy of the Absurd is a philosophy of the rich which they require the poor to live. Beckett has just written a couple of pages which can be bought for a thousand pounds a time. That is an act of violence.

It seemed to me that violence was made inherent in our way of life. I dont think we're born animals with a natural need to be violent. We're born full of history. We come with the battles of many generations in us. Our hands are plans drawn by human societies. We come to the world as people, not animals. We inherit violence socially - not biologically. Violence is a practical philosophy - like language. We have the physiological capacity to speak and part of our brain is designated for speaking. But we learn to speak. And our language isnt created in the brain and never was. It was created in social intercourse and then taught to - put in - the brain. And it's so with the ways of violence. If the part of the brain devoted to speaking is not educated (by the process of learning language) it remains inert - it does not seek to invent a language. I think that inevitably children will produce aggressive behaviour - but this does not have to be philosophised into a way of life - as it is in much of our education, art, modes of living. We now have a government openly encouraging selfishness and aggression.

It follows from all this that in many ways I will deal with violence. Technically I try to make violence unglamourous and dramatically impelling. I sometimes talk of aggro-effects - effects designed to make the audience question what they normally accept - but this isnt to shock them pointlessly.[1] I place the violence in a context which makes the violence a riddle - with obvious social analogies (the stoning in *Saved*) - or illuminating, revealing (the stripping of the parson in *The Fool*, where even when he's stripped of his social uniform his naked flesh is stolen goods, looted from the poor and defenceless). The important point is always the questions the violence leads to. I hope these remarks are useful.

About the Dublin production of *Human Cannon*.[2] I think the actors will have the advantage of experiences gained in the Manchester production.[3] Of course this will enable them to understand the characters more fully. But perhaps even more important it will enable the actors to make tactically more useful

---

[1] For further information on "aggro-effects" see Edward Bond and Christopher Innes', "Edward Bond; From Rationalism to Rhapsody,"*Canadian Theatre Review* 23, (Summer 1979) and Peter Holland, "Brecht, Bond, Gaskill and the Practice of Political Theatre" *Theatre Quarterly*, Vol. VIII, 30 (1978).

[2] Bond wrote *Human Cannon* in 1983 for Yvonne Bryceland. The Dublin production was in 1989. More production information can be found in Edward Bond's Letters, volume 2, Gordon & Breach.

[3] Quantum Theatre, Manchester, produced the play on 5 July, 1986.

decisions about how to portray the characters. We still think that we can collapse the performance into the reality of the characters. But suppose we say: this character is greedy. That doesnt tell us how to portray the greed. The actual way of portraying anything is always social - otherwise the actor would have to be playing him or herself. But if the actor plays the character, the actor cant just magically become the character. The actor has to choose how to become it. So the actor might say: this action is *good*. He has to show the action in a certain way. I repeat, to do something in a stage area is an artificial thing and cannot be derived directly from the motive for doing it: if a real person really does something in a real room, then the real action proceeds directly from the real motive. The real person has no choice - once he has made his free-will decision. But suppose I want to show on stage that someone has or has not got free will. The decision still wont show me how to show it. It's in this sense that all stage actions are in some sense outside the character's control or choosing. We think we can use the action to show the character. But this is circular - since we've just said that the character does X because he is that character. So the social always intervenes in the stage - nothing can be collapsed into its real self. That is the advantage of showing anything on stage - because it takes the common social process (that we're all socially constructed, cultured, developed) and isolates it twice over: the theatre itself is a specific social activity with conventions and practical necessities that re-impose the social when in our automatic day-to-day living it may become lost to our own awareness. This isnt a matter of choice. Decide: my character would do this - but you still have to decide precisely how he will do it. The character fact cant dictate the action. The character might dictate: kill X. But it cant dictate: how do I show X being killed or me killing X. That has to be a further stage. And even if I really did kill X - I would still have to show the killing. A rope - an axe - falling from a cliff: these are all ways of showing death, making it visual. If I do it behind a high wall at Wormwood Scrubs I will show it in a notice shortly after attached to the prison gate; showing death - part of the act of killing - will include jerking someone on the end of a rope - and hanging up a placard as if I were putting a picture on the wall. It cannot - none of these things - can happen invisibly. They are all matters of choice - not intention: and they all describe a social context. So a character must always speak language which isnt his own (on the stage) and make movements which arent his own - and cannot be: anymore than the puppet's movements are its own. This means that we can always socially interpret the play and then decide how to show anything: and the showing is the thing by which we are judged - because it is our way of judging what we show. If I write a play then I tell the truth about the people. That doesnt decide how the truth is shown: it is merely part of the showing - it defines the general area. But the actor must choose - must find ways of clarifying. Always when an actor says he's being, interpreting, the character, he is really judging the character: the fact is that the character does nothing to the actor and the actor does everything to the character. So it might be that at some time I would want to show an action as quiet and at another time - in another production - show the same action as quick - or smooth whereas before it was angular - or in one production point at Y and in another at X. This wouldnt change the immediate meaning (a stone is a stone is a stone) but would change the social meaning (this stone you thought was in a prison is in a school). Even if you understood the character you wouldnt know how to play it. The character is there (I put it provocatively) to understand you - to show what you are. But really: in the space between the character and the actor - the space filled by the performance - the audience is able to see itself or come face to face with itself (which isnt of course the same as seeing). The character merely dies, loves, eats, sins, is heroic: we have to show the meaning of these things - not, I repeat, choose to give them a meaning: we cannot do them unless we apply a meaning to them - but as we're not usually self-questioning we think the meanings are automatic. Literally, they cant be: they're either taught - or, if we act freely, learned.

You're right that I did say the personal ambitions of the players in the RSC *War Plays* interfered with their work.[4] I should have said not merely, not always ambitions, but also fears and insecurities. The working situation was very badly set up - for which I was responsible. But it was an attempt to get the play on. I shouldnt have made the attempt in that way. I think the Manchester production worked because the space between the actor and the character wasnt filled with ambition or fear, but with a social concern: so things were not reduced to their physical tensions and dynamics - as if a human act were equivalent to a plate falling from a table. The integrity of a community was put on stage - and so actions became aesthetically accurate, shocking and beautiful: the meaning was put into the action and these qualities were found in that way. Normally it's done the other way round: love scene - soft music - anger - noisy music. Or worse:

---

[4] The complete production of the *War Plays* was in the RSC repertoire from 17 July, 1985.

anger - alienate it with soft music. Any accurate description of anything usually contains contradictions.

You point out that I say in the preface to *Lear* that "If we do not stop being violent we have no future" but in *War Plays* I show survivors of a nuclear hyper-holocaust (to inflate language) creating a future.[5] Well, the Woman becomes the foundation of the community by going away from it - a monitory foundation. I suppose if the community took up violence - either because it put the individual before society, or a God before the individual - then those survivors would destroy themselves. That is the Woman's meaning.

Perhaps I ought to return to my earlier point. An actor might say: I agree I cannot do X in the real way the character (if real) would do X - but I can show you how that character would do it - and derive the way of showing it, doing it, from the character: thus, the character in effect does it to the actor. The character is being the actor. Well of course the writer is doing something like this when he writes the character: he lets the character be itself on the stage (a line from Falstaff isnt a line from Hamlet). The space between the writer and the character is that the writer chooses the situation in which he puts the character (or allows this to be dictated to him by convention, misprision, ignorance, etc.). He chooses the way of telling the incident. Show the murder - show the consequence - show a passerby during the murder - etc. So the action cant be shown - by the actor - as one in a "life series" - but only as one in a play series. So it must relate to a preselection of actions - a story series. This means that the actor cannot help but have to play - tell - judge - the story - and not merely "obey" his character. The actor searches for the character - tries to find it. I want to say, however, that there is always a space - and that the actor must choose how he fills the space. The actor may say he receives a creative joy in being the character: but I think the joy is really in showing (there is an audience) the character. Of course there is an element of being in performance: but performance isnt the same as being. And the being in the performance is not the character but the showing; performing the showing. So what the actor is doing is actually taking the "way of showing" as being itself the character - and that he finds creative satisfaction in performing the characteristics (perhaps in series). He would then have to treat the characteristics (requirements) of the stage in the same automatic way: the stage has characteristics in the same ways that characters have characteristics. And the

---

5 "Preface to 'Lear'" *Bond: Plays Two*, London: Methuen, 1978. 3.

audience is bound to respond to them automatically. But then I dont see how any human action could have meaning - our minds would be operating like physical things. Certainly such an actor would imagine that he was involved in precisely the opposite - finding the authentic soul of his character, for instance. But this doesnt seem to correspond with all the elaborate social institutions of theatre. Couldnt all this be got from a sports field? We seem to want to put on stage precisely those things we dont understand - and cant handle by playing the rules of a game. We seem to be examining the rules. A goal is a goal: an act isnt an act. Even if the actor "reproduces the character's essentiality" he has to reproduce it within a series of conventions and restrictions which are social-geographic (a stage is as specific to an audience as a dock is to a court of law). And so the performance is always out of the character's hands. It's as if there were a bag full of groceries. These are the character. The stage must spill the contents of the bag. How they are picked up is in fact the performance. So the stage insists on social observation and not merely reproduction. But we then have to ask why societies have stages: the reason changes historically according to the way we see ourselves and how we live. The space is filled differently. It is always created by the character. The audience are there because they need the space. It's in the space that the actor and audience meet and from there they observe the character.

So the actor is free to choose - and still "be" the character. The character could choose his characteristic way of performing an act in real life - but it wouldnt be the same way that it would be done on stage: wouldnt and couldnt be. The real person does it, the actor tells it: telling fills the space and the audience have come to see what's in the space and not the character (the audience does that when it looks round at itself).

There is another problem. A writer assumes that the way of filling the space will be the socially useful one - that it will, in that way, tell the truth. Shakespeare believed in the reality of ghosts. We dont. Shakespeare chooses a story-series which he imagines to relate to a real-series in a certain way. But since we understand reality differently, we have to create a new series - a sort of story within the story - which we put into the space. Otherwise we speak of a permanent human nature. This means that when we go to the theatre we would happily walk under the severed heads on London Bridge as Shakespeare's public did. A natural event has no meaning for us till we make it into a social event: if society changes we change, because we apprehend nature - our's included - differently. But a modern writer will hope to make the space productive in a new way - in accord with the way society now lives. We do not need ghosts to understand ourselves - they become a confusion. Hamlet needed them. I suppose we can say his space was haunted. Our space is filled with the dead of Belsen - with hands of hungry people - with our fear of streets, not ghosts. The audience puts its world into that space: and the actor must play the audience - or play out the fulfillment of its need.

I hope these remarks are useful.

Regards,

Edward Bond

Patricia A Bond
Egham, Surrey   15 March 1989

Dear Ms. Bond,

        Thanks for your letter. I set *Narrow Road* in an Oriental aesthetic because
it's a form of alienation: it enables one to see more clearly things that can be
muddied by their immediacy. I got the idea from Voltaire's contes - especially
the moment when someone describes the tracks made in the dust by a dog (did
Poe read this before he created Auguste Dupin?). It isolates moral questions from
immediate assumptions and therefore from prejudices. Alienations ought to be
the opposite from aesthetics - they ought to heighten perception. But not in the
sense that drugs (hallucinogens) do this because they obscure reality by putting
imagination in front of it - instead of seeing it as a foundation.

        About directing and acting. Actors are encouraged to acquire
performance skills - and to interpret characters in terms of their psychology. I
understand why they interpret in this way and acknowledge that there is certainly
something called psychological truth to a character - and that one creates this
when writing a character. But a character can't on the stage be reduced to its
psychology. This is because there is what I call a gap between the character, the
actor, and the audience. Given that the character does something characteristic,
this nevertheless doesn't determine how the action is performed. Taking
something from a real room or street and putting it on the stage means adding an
extra dimension to the action. This is derived from two sources. One is the
geography of the stage - the act must be seen (obviously a murderer isn't
concerned with showing his act to an audience). This distorts the real action into
stage action. Secondly, why are the audience there? They have come to a
showing. This isn't a purely physiological matter but a social matter: what, for
them, is the purpose of theatre? This varies historically with the individual's
relation to society and vice versa. Really this gap is an area dedicated to
philosophy - and it's where, for example, theatrical (or any artistic) style becomes
itself a signifier. But nothing can be reduced to its signifiers. It would seem that
the story carries the philosophy of the piece. But this would be a false reduction.
You would have to ask, does the story tell the language or does the language tell
the story? You would think that the story uses language to tell itself. But
grammar itself contains, to put it crudely, meaning - it donates values etc. A

story can appear in many cultures (obviously this is true of many myths and of many newspaper reports) but have different meanings in those languages. So it's as if there were one meaning which is very close to the grammar in which it is expressed. However, one reason why people have art is to question their culture - the very grammar of their existence. Even if they wish to confirm that culture they must analyse it in moments of art. This is because, although grammar is permanent and holistic (it is idiom, slang, technicalese which change) nevertheless, art must interrogate its grammar - because people ask basic questions. Naturally, grammar cannot be penetrated - and so we always speak a stranger's language. Then why alienate - when we are already so alienated in social practice and ontologically? In order to understand ourselves. This sounds very abstract - what it means in the theatre is that audiences go there (that is, are sent there by their society) in order to replace psychology with philosophy. Human psychology is merely a convention - acquired before we have any social competence. It originates in our infancy and is socially taught. Children ask holistic philosophical questions - not "What is a fork?" but "Why is it a fork?" The questions are true, but they can only be answered, on the infant's level, by lies. So our quest for truth must be met with lies - that is a consequence of being human. It doesn't make any sense to say that the foundation of a dog's psychology is lies - but it's true of human beings since the human brain is interrogatory and holistic, not sectioned into instincts. Really the human need for art comes from the fact that we're born infants - and it leads to the nice paradox that all art is founded in lies. That's why it's important to say that art is intellectual and a search for truth - rational.

The experience - often painful - of earlier generations becomes - through culture impressed in organisation, technology, and grammar - the psychology of later generations. That process will become more conscious as human beings interpret their relationship to the world more and more truthfully (or at least practically - but then practicality must have a moral content). So the function of art changes. The work of art in a prehistoric cave, an Egyptian temple, a Greek temple, a modern city remains the same. I recognise in early cave paintings that the maker intended to produce something I call art. But the purpose for which he created it is very different from the use *I* make of it. So the audience (sent to theatre by its society) uses theatre arts differently in differing stages of history. Really it's always been a question of substituting philosophy for psychology - and in later times that philosophy then becomes integral to psychology (though remembering that the child must be told lies. A child must be housed in the world so you tell it of Father Christmas - who wears, incidentally, the red and white of martyrdom. If you told the child of relativity or superforce, you would dehouse it in the world).

So any strange action must tell the story - the story doesn't tell the action (at the most, it only partly does so). But the story can't be reduced to characterisations - that the story exists as it is because the characters are what they are, is wrong. The gap has to be filled with philosophy - this shows how the action is to be performed and also the meaning of the action. My reservation about Brecht is that he seems to think that an action can be divorced from all values and seen objectively: as if, perhaps, you found the meaning of a sentence by reducing it to its grammar - instead of its social context. But of course people assume that this is what Brecht *is* doing. Brecht doesn't, however, do this - he incorporates Marxism as a positive value on stage. I've no objection to this - except that he lets Marxist philosophy preselect what happens on stage, deleting what is not amenable to immediate action. Then why does Mother Courage stop to watch a woman washing her hair - and not her hands?

Yours sincerely,

Edward Bond

Chapter Two

Theatre Events (TEs)

Moshen Baraket
University of Kent
Canterbury, Kent   3 February 1990

Dear Moshen Baraket,

By TEs I may mean something a bit different from what you call "theatricality." I don't think meaning adheres in our life even to the limited extent it did in the past. If an ideology - say a religion - is very strong that means its supports and explains an economy and a state administration, or accommodates its criticisms to these things as the Orthodox Church did in czarist Russia for example: then the people do in fact begin to live the religion: thus it may support, say, a minor-capitalist economy but at the same time provide opportunities for monks, hermits, mystics who "withdraw" from the economy. Forms of repression are then able to provide at the same time a humanistic - and humanizing - tinge: the scythe is used to scatter the seeds. The people live uniform patterns. Then art can be stated in terms of known icons. Christian art is an obvious example - or say the painting of medieval China, where landscape denies any political, economic terrain. That form of mysticism disappears from the heavily Chinese-influenced Japanese art during the eighteenth century: in the great ukiyoe prints farmers bend their backs, carpenters saw, porters carry heavy burdens, ships fight storms - it is the world of successful entrepreneurs. The print makers combine a visionary statement of people's life with great practicality. I don't think this sort of art exists now because people's lives have no immediate meaning: there is no human or divine purpose. Obviously this creates problems for playwrights and actors: it's a matter of literally knowing what they are setting out to do when they write and act - and also why the audience wants them to do these things. Obviously audiences are happy to be entertained in a way that removes the problem rather than solves it: because any solution makes a demand on them. Yet it is not merely in the more general interest of the audience that the problems are solved: it is also, I think, a psychological desire or need of theirs. I don't want at the moment to go into too much detail as to why this is so. I think its to do with the way people first create consciousness - how they become aware of certain relations in the world: the child has the problem of learning to speak, of growing up: so its problems are those of "learning to be." It arrives at solutions which are at the same time its conception of what its doing: the child has to conceive the world. Once started, the process can't be stopped - except through gross psychological degeneration and probably not even then. It's the area I've touched on in some of the notes in the PM plays. It means that consciousness is always involved in drama, that being conscious is itself a dramatic form. The theatre is able to deal in a privileged way with the situations which entail drama - it examines them critically, and at the same time it enables the audience to live them through surrogates.

What would happen in Christian art (mostly music and pictorial) is that the "self-drama" would be exposed and reinterpreted in terms of the ruling ideology - which incorporated the moral and the intellectual. This can't happen in the postmodern world because there is no prevailing coherent ideology which satisfies both the state (economy and administration) and the psyche: hence, for example, the absurdist doctrine that nothing has meaning - or the nihilist doctrine that nothing has value. So that art, which frequently has been used to express the most idealised values - is then used to cast them down: the same ability - art - does two opposing things - because art has to be a statement of truth as it is seen to be (the values don't lie in the art itself, except that they are an ability to pose questions and formulate answers systematically). The present situation in the West is that the state can no longer teach any reason for existing: say what the purpose of human life is. Yet it's the purpose of art to define that purpose - in strenuous or rewarding terms (that is because consciousness is a drama). If there is an adherence to the shell of the state, then art adopts nihilism/absurdity - perhaps with a gesture to residual resources in human beings, the ability to change - this is said to be the justification of Beckett. But resources only lie at the end of tragedy - after the tragic act: that is, Hamlet acts - and then gestures to the meaninglessness beyond acting/action - he does not claim to be either God or even God's agent: he merely acts to correct a misalignment of the state (ultimately, for Shakespeare, this does point towards a divine assurance of human value, because the state-and-people are seen as reflections of the divine). We cannot have meaning in this way: we cannot incorporate the story into the events to give them meaning - at the most the story will point to cause-and-effect but not to meaning, purpose, or value. The story does not give the stage of the story meaning.

It's to achieve this meaning that I use TEs. The acting cannot be reduced to the character and not even to the story. Macbeth sees a knife in the air. The knife for Shakespeare is a projection of Macbeth's mind - and perhaps also of the witches (this is Shakespeare's pointing to the ultimate supernaturality of his world). In *Woyzeck*, the knife used to murder Marie is bought from a Jew (Berg doesn't use this scene in his opera: if he did the big orchestral interlude before the final scene would sound comic - because it points to a psychological realm which the play itself is fighting to deny). How would we use the knife now? Each of the three knives are "real" - but each has an historical limitation. If I use ghosts I don't use Shakespeare's. Indeed, my ghosts have to die - or (another group of them) they are dead in order that they may succeed in (the state's version of) life. So the strategy of TEs is: we select incidents in the story and open these incidents out in such a way that they can't be captured by the story but must be examined for themselves in relation to the story: then "reality" may impose its interpretation on the story. Of course I write in such a way not merely to make this possible - but to demand it. I think that is the stumbling block the present theatre has with my work. I think TEs should be used to act and direct all plays, however ancient: then we can see what they meant for their creators and how they can have meaning for us.

Is there a tension between the TEs and the story? The story must have a psychological-emotional colour: or else everything is said in the third person and people are reduced to matchstick men, as in early Piscator. But this creates a form, not a content. Language is situated in emotion: so the use of any language in a dramatic text must create a specific structure. You normally say "and so they married and lived happily ever after" not "and so they married and lived happily for the next five minutes." But if the text has a structure - and emotional tempo and ambience - won't taking it apart in the TEs destroy this: and won't the actor be lost - like someone playing the drums in the hope of making the sound of a piano? And also, structures are built into the actor and his relation to the character: the relationships aren't arbitrary. To be true to the character, the actor must impose this truth on text. So to use TEs and the text properly ought not to be possible. I can only say it is - and that the TEs illuminate and do not destroy the text. Perhaps this is for a very profound reason: that the story turns specifically on points of conflict in the telling - and not merely on their resolution. Thus we have to gather certain events together in order to make a story; and the end imposes interpretations on the series of events. Of course, this is part convention (the audience knows what the events are supposed to mean) - and part surprise. And it really is just these events which are being wrongly captured by the story and forced into ideological conformity: hence the arbitrariness of classic endings - these tend to cheat the audience because they pretend to live their life for them: "they lived happily ever after" - is a lie being offered to the audience, as if the actors could live away their (the audience's) problems. And Hamlet's death is not (normally) a way to live. I suppose people will always live in tension between the real determinate structures of their lives (factories, banks, museums are not part of our skeleton - yet we base our lives on them, they're part of our interior) and what they must do as part of their practical life. The area of tension is the field of art. It must be kept (for us) rational and not mystified. I find that in practice, provided the actors understand what is happening, TEs become a way of expressing the character - but perhaps in a heightened way. Subjectivity isn't abandoned - but is made objective (as indeed I believe it to be in all real crises and profound involvements: what we usually call "subjectivity" is just shorthand for not being there - or for the frenzy that occurs when we wholly live the ideology). The art and skill of theatre should lie in exploiting TEs. This brings it very close to what I think you mean by theatricality but that is an abstract theatricality. Such an abstraction would be like performance art - trying to find meaning in pure physicality - often in disturbed forms. Thus smearing the naked body with paint and them painting the walls. I have nothing much against this except when it claims to tell us why walls are built, who owns them, who climbs them to escape, and who is shot on them. There is a difference between paint on walls and soldier's blood running down walls - as Blake makes clear. And as "happenings" confuse.

I'll try to answer some of your specific questions. I saw *Camino Real* very early - probably before I'd written *Pope's Wedding*. I like its plasticity. But I felt it was wayward in that Williams confused his obsessions with facts. He is interested in the body as a barrier: thus the heart that's searched for is really an organ inside the body. The soul in *Grandma Faust* is social. I am interested in the extended, social body. Soul is a metaphysical concept. Romantics search for the heart (well, minor romantics do). Black people are interested in soul because for them it has political connotations - it denotes their strength to act as political agents. You own your heart (unless you give it away in personal love). The soul is never yours - it signifies a relationship with something external. I think the concept of soul has limited aesthetic uses. In *A-A-America* there is a journey from the buying of souls to the coin tossed on the ground as an indicator of the destruction of bodies. I don't think that interested Williams. He told me that he liked the second half of *The Woman* because it was for him more personal: fishing people, an island, a race. (In the second half I tried to create a political symbolic scheme - the Woman really represents the life of many hundreds of years: but I've written about all that elsewhere). He couldn't respond to the first half because war and peace were too abstract for him. The great war for him would be the American Civil War. Can you imagine him writing a play about Vietnam? One of his last works is about a woman who's interned in a private mad house - she comes out on a trial-freedom and gets upset - and she's threatened with being put in the state asylum (not her private one) which she's told would be much much worse. But I would want to write about the state asylum - I think that is what a writer ought to do. The extended social body would then be more revealing, very often. Even in *The Sea.* I haven't read Jasper's *Tragedy is not Enough.* Or I have forgotten reading it.

The question of using plays in plays, in which the stage-audiences participate. Why don't I write so that the real audience can participate in the same way? The play within the play in Shakespeare is often the dramatising of the subjective. My p's-within-the-p are, I think, always objective. So for the theatre audience they dramatise the way to use the play: they show the structure of the plays, and their relation to the audience. I think workshops are very useful - and forms of group theatre where audiences can fully involve themselves. But a member of the audience, though he or she might have an intense experience in these situations, doesn't generalise (necessarily) that experience. A lot of group work can be fairly reactionary. I suppose that writing a play is a way of avoiding this. It's a grey area. I can't play a musical instrument (pace Stockhausen saying we all can) but I like listening to musical instruments being played. Watching very good actors is in itself a pleasure. But it's the relation of the actor to the audience which is important. The actors can be my social self. (I thought the question was very interesting.)

Do I write for specific stages? I imagine that I had the R[oyal] C[ourt] stage in mind for most of my early work. You point out the fishing scene in *Saved* as being evidence of this. That's certainly true - but the scene could also work with the actor's back to the audience and the rod pointing away from them. I think that television has made audiences very expert in the handling of space - more so than most contemporary actors and directors. If you stage *The Woman* in a small space then you affect the play because it's epic size is clear. It's a bit like going to the seaside for a holiday but then never going to the sea and instead staying inside the hotel. But the insides of hotels have their uses.

The habit of changing scenery before the audience - increasing the light for the change instead of decreasing it, is another matter.[1] It's like allowing "dead" actors to stand and walk off.[2] This is deliberately done to reassure the audience of the theatrical nature of the stage - that if it becomes an illusion beyond the willing suspension of belief then it loses much of its value. The reality of the stage is far greater than that created by the mere suspension of belief. The stage deals with the audience's extended body - the social self: it's in real life that the audience tends to practice suspension of belief about this - and they don't notice it. Making the stage clearly a stage lets it enter into areas of reality which are normally excluded from the audience's immediate awareness - although it is their reality, their social self. So if the theatre is a social machine, these other areas become available to it. I suppose an audience in real life constantly suspends and apprehends belief, constantly contacts and loses reality. What is the area of belief when Mary Whitehouse thinks she sees God? Or a Soviet dissident believes he saw the Virgin Mary floating over a building and claims that a crowd of several thousand saw her? What is the level of belief when you see soldiers as heroes going to recapture the Falkland Islands? The self is a drama of many stages: the stage shouldn't be allowed to hide away in mere pretence.

When I speak of the stage as a stage I mean a stage in society. I don't think that society can't be changed. Obviously it always changes anyway. But I

---

[1] Increasing the lighting intensity in scene changes has been a practice in most of Bond's productions.

[2] An example was Yvonne Bryceland as Marthe who, in the 1982 National Theatre production of *Summer*, walked off stage after her character's death occurred.

think it can be changed by social political action and by artistic means. The two have to go together. All revolutions create a new aesthetic. Stalin reimposed an old aesthetic: social realism - invented by the nineteenth century as an escape from romantic evasions. Though of course Cervantes was already a realist: the lions in the cage bring the fable elements in other parts of *Don Quixote* into absolute realism - notice how one becomes aware of the street on which the cage is standing. We need a theatre which doesn't escape into mere performance and happenings - but can deal with the relation between the stage-drama and the ego-drama and involves itself in that area of tension and adaptation which constantly exists between the two. If the stage doesn't do this, it becomes a ghetto, and its function is taken over by other aesthetic elements in society - but not necessarily in an interrogating, creative way. The prototype play is *Oedipus* - not because of the specific nature of his problem but because it shows how the actor creates a past from the present. Of course the Greeks then see the past as determinant - but in the relation of the two dramas, as I understand it, it is exactly the discourse between the present and the past which gives us our freedom provided the discourse is interrogative.

Madness. I don't object to Shakespeare's using Lear's madness as the way of telling insights. I think that's the only way a writer of Shakespeare's age could tell them. (As a writer, Shakespeare lacks the shocking modernity of, say, Winstanley - but he has been more potent because he relied on God less.) I think Nietzsche's madness has its cause in that he's taken thought as far as someone like him could. Nietzsche was a psychologist and the themes this gave him drove him mad: he was driven mad by reflecting on the nature of reason. Marx in fact thinks beyond Nietzsche. But isn't there partial truth in the idea that Lenin saw the party elite as supermen and superwomen? - or found them being put in these roles after 1917? Marx however was not a psychologist and his statistics saved him from madness (well, the statistics and Hegel's example as a conceptualiser). Both dealt with great movements of history and saw that the social body was still alien to the self. Nietzsche wanted a self that would transcend (or in his physical training mood, dominate) the social body. Marx understood rightly that there could only be peace when the two were as near one as they can be when the relation is somewhat like that between the leaf and the tree. But in practice - it's the record of communist rule - the self-drama was discounted: and then reality becomes unreal and dangerous. I should add to what I said above about TEs. The relationship to the text is profound because TEs are not (it turns out in practice) imposed on moments of the story - but are drawn from them, they are already naturally there once anyone undertakes to tell any story. So then the emotional-psychological line of the story - which absolutely has its own character - isn't destroyed: it appears to be cast quite rigidly, but it's exactly this rigidity which gives it its flexibility. A loosely written line or incident is like a piece of damp string - it wavers all over the place and has in itself no real shape. The rigidly exact line (whether in Shakespeare, Racine, Euripides) is precisely the one that smashes into its fragments when struck and seen to an assembly of usable flaws. This is true of a line as well as of a dramatic unit, or moment, or confrontation. One reason why I left the RSC production of the *War Plays* is that I found the actors - who wanted to escape from the artificial concepts of directors ("Lets do it in regency") wanted instead to get back to the theatre of someone like Irving, using the stage as if it were a concrete area with its own all-determining rules.

In rehearsal, I tend to place a great reliance of the words - at the beginning. Cicely Berry at the RSC begins very much with the words: letting the actors speak, sound, move, be moved by the words - getting the words' kinesthetic qualities before their abstract qualities.[3] Abstractions are after all only attempts to make the physical manipulable. I wouldn't find a disagreement between this approach and my own. The actor should be fuelled with the language because that's going to be his lifeline in performance. But what I think surprising is that this doesn't capture the actor but liberates him into being able to choose his creative use of the kinesthetic-presence. It's this which energizes the TEs. I hope these remarks are of some use to you.

Best wishes,

Edward Bond

---

[3] Cicely Berry is the Voice Director for the Royal Shakespeare Company.

John Clemo

London, NW9   12 February 1990

Dear John Clemo,

The performance you saw of *Jackets* was a bit disappointing.[1] I'd seen the dress rehearsal and that had been a much better performance. The actors had put in so much effort that when the play came together at the dress rehearsal they seemed to have become exhausted - so that the play didnt develop in the short run, but seemed rather to be repeating itself mechanically. A pity. But I was very grateful to them. I remember that I'd wondered whether the play's dual structure would hold together - and I'd had an unexpected sense of elucidation watching the performance: a feeling of calmness, because the relation between the late medieval Japanese mountain village and the twentieth century city of high rise blocks, seemed so clear. I dont suppose I shall see the whole play again - with a company of children as well as the adults. *Jackets II* (the second half) is being revised at the Bush Theatre later this month. The second half works on its own.[2]

I wanted to direct *Cannon* at the N[ational]T[heatre] with Yvonne Bryceland playing Agustina. Hall asked me to direct it there with Vanessa Redgrave in the part. I refused. There've been several amateur productions. It's meant to be produced in Glasgow later this year by a young people's theatre company.[3]

I suppose the distinction between problem and answer plays breaks down in these changing times. To state the problem clearly is necessarily part of the answer. Leninism has failed to found itself in the popular will. There is a curious difficulty in its structure. Up until the time of capitalism there was an ideological unity between leaders and led. God spoke and all people were subject to his authority. The prince might have earthly power but the poor had as much right (and often more) to divine succour as he did. Unity broke down when society's relation to "nature" was changed by technology. Instead of the Bible the law book, the "instructions for use," the technical drawings, became decisive - and

---

[1] Bond is referring to a complete production of *Jackets* at the Nuffield Studio, Lancaster University, 24-26 January, 1989.

[2] In subsequent conversations Bond has stated the need for the staging of the entire play.

[3] The 1990 production of *Human-Cannon* was directed in Glasgow by Nick Philippou.

creative. So there was a specialist elite created: the soul has no specialisms, the intellect does. How to bridge the new division? Nietzsche wanted supermen who treated the proletariate as scum. Lenin wanted a super party who would be the emancipators of the proletariate. Every "soul" can be equally good: but the intellect is a matter of learning - goodness of attitude, perhaps. So how is knowledge to be made effective? - that's the new problem. But knowledge doesnt work abstractly - it's entangled with psychology and practice. In 1917 spontaneous (more or less) groups appeared called Soviets. Instead of the Soviets giving vitality to the party - the party had its own disciplines, ladders of access, etc. - and people trained in these party-ways then took over the other organisations. Knowledge then has no psychological existence - doesnt become part of the wear and tear and refinement and strengthening of practice. Its vitality becomes authoritarian and restrictive.

What's the relationship of this to aesthetics? Political theatre has tended to work from the standpoint of the party: it has tried to *give* knowledge to the group (the Soviet or the people in the street). It has discounted psychology. But it's only when analytical knowledge becomes psychological practice that knowledge takes on the characteristics of (almost) revelation: it works. This is why we now have to move on from the alienation-effect and its correlates: they're founded on the Lenin division of the problem. This stage was inevitable - after all, it did end the internecine warring in Europe - till capitalism (through Hitler) brought it back again. Instead of the A-effect we need something I call Theatre Events - TEs. These show how scenes are to be directed and characters played. The events of the story are used in such a way that instead of being alienated merely - seen without their traditional prejudgments - they're integrated into the production of psychology. I'll try to explain this briefly and simply. Imagine a poem in which someone says to a hungry woman: All you need is a bowl of soup and the works of Lenin. There is actually a Brecht poem which says something much like this. It seems to me a good (in both senses) example of the A-effect. It's shocking to give a starving woman and her baby a book. Yet it means: you need food to live, but also to live (not be bombed, not have your child's brain destroyed by pollution) you need an analytical understanding of your situation. I cant disagree with this. Earlier people would have said: she needs soup and the Bible. But both of these statements seem to me to inherit an aesthetics based on the estrangement between party and Soviet, between church and people, ideology and religious practice. The church was wiser because it connected the soul with psychology - you see this clearly in its art. The party (at its worst) discounted psychology: knowledge was pure - and might be handed over in pure forms. Say to suggest one way of showing this, on stage the woman sat with her child and a bowl of soup - and then behind her on a screen in large letters would appear pages from the works of Lenin. You are left with the problem of connecting the two - the audience are left with that dilemma: they see the truth being stated but dont know how it's integrated in their lives. The well-intended ideas of the party might be engraved on stone. Whatever is engraved on stone - not "written in flesh" - tends to become a gravestone: it's sterile - except perhaps in emergencies, because then all things are simplified. But that's not a guide to normal living or coherent change. To make of this (deliberately chosen, and therefore artificial and tendentious) example of A-effect into a TE, the book and the soup must appear on the same plane. Naturalism and realism - the event and its analysis - mustnt be divorced. The actor doesnt play the frightened weak woman nursing the baby with the soup - she must have the book. Does she give the baby a spoonful of soup - then read aloud (perhaps she cant read well) one sentence? Then how true, relevant, simple, earth-shattering, is the sentence? Does it become more important than the soup - perhaps the soup is put down and she reads the text to herself and the child as if it were a fairy story that had become true? Perhaps soup is spilt on the book - perhaps the child cries each time the spoon is taken from its mouth as the woman uses it to painfully underline the text. Perhaps someone comes on and kicks the soup away - and thrusts the book in her hand: and tells her she and her child will die if they dont understand the book. All these possibilities belong in the realm of TE. A line - a scene - part of a scene - all of these can be used as TEs. The aim is to theatricalise the analysis. Of course Brecht himself often does this - so does Dante and Cervantes. You cant write well without doing it. But *we* have this advantage: that we can read new knowledge into the analysis - into the theatricalisation. That it seems to me is what aesthetics should be doing. "Happenings" try to reduce theatre to things that have value in themselves. But this is a form of mysticism - and that means of psychological submission (I mean that quite technically - as masochism is a technical adjustment of the psyche faced with certain problems). Or else to some form of socio-biology. But aesthetics are integral to the working of the brain precisely because they look at the instinctive in a way which is interrogative and speculative: and which then becomes a particular society's form of knowledge. For example, you could not have gods - and religion - unless the mind were aesthetical.   You could not tell a story - or construct a theology, because theologies are derivative from stories.   Aesthetics dont create a basic, natural, instinctive realm.   Different societies use aesthetics differently - and have to: a sailor's tattoos work differently from those of a bushman's.   Mrs. Beeton's cookery book - a highly aestheticised work as you can gather from the title - is different from the aesthetics of the canning industry (which actually often prostitutes Mrs. Beeton).   The gods in Greek theatre are different from the Puritan god who condemned theatre - but they had witch burning spectacles (happenings?).   In our society ad men use aesthetics to change behaviour - and this means to change consciousness, to integrate the illustration into the text of daily practice.   I think that aesthetically people create themselves in forms of tension - outside the assurance of a self-developing society and the assurance of the seasons.   Human psychology is dramatic because of the way a child learns language and behaviour in relation to vastly superior powers but with a will of its own.   The split between will and knowledge.   But I cant go into that here!

The point is that now people create their psyche in a new way.   Yet theatre wants to create character in an Ibsenite way - or a wholly alienated way, which divorces psychology from practice (this wasnt at all Brecht's intention but it's the common understanding of him).   In theatre, we can open up both the situation and the character(s) to form TEs - which in effect reproduce the pattern people are actually living, but do so in a way in which they can be examined.   Nothing has value on the stage till it's put in its context.   (Happenings presuppose that things do have value -that there is a positive mystical alienation.)   I dont think art has ever reproduced ("just like life," "she *was* the character she played!") but has produced.   That's its cerebral function - its connection with mind.   When cinema was invented it wasnt used merely to reproduce naturalism.   The passengers werent shown going on a normal train journey.   The train was shown narrowly missing the car on the level crossing.   Nor were film characters "natural" - the great film performers were *alienators*: Keyton's face - and whoever saw anyone like Chaplin?   These actions were accompanied by someone in the pit playing a piano (music compensates for the lack of a third dimension on the screen).   The pianist is naturally alienating.   He provides fast music for the chase, mood music for the love scene, but each is usually "appropriate" (with ironic interventions) to bourgeois sensibility.   In opera, music and singer are one: they are involved in the same action - that's partly why Wagner wanted to hide the orchestra.   But the pit pianist in the cinema needs to see - because performer and music werent "one" but estranged. The orchestra belonged to the singer (opera), the pit pianist to the cinema audience. With talkies something changed. The alienated silent figure vanished (consider Chaplin's return to "naturalism"). This meant that film music then became like opera music - it belonged to the performer. But the performer spoke (unlike the opera singer: though you can reflect on sprech-gesang - the intoned speaking used by Schönberg and Berg etc - who wished to escape from the unity of singer-music). This was potentially reactionary - because the musical commentary disappeared into the speaker - like a socio-biological instinct. No alienation then: but the emotion (music) could not even be examined. This really was a further development of the Wagner gesamnt kunstwerk. Now the music does not alienate or even comment - but instructs. Of course much music does in fact comment, but in the dramatic moments - the moments of meaning and value - the music is internalised and imposes value and meaning. The audience are not free - except by detaching themselves critically from the film - to acquire knowledge: it's a knee-jerk coming from the brain. To help you to understand this a bit more Im sending you some notes I recently made about the use of music in *Restoration*.[4] On the West End stage now there is a revival in the musical. The British musical has achieved some importance: this is because it dealt with more political subjects - taboo in America except by import - but used music (as in films) to imprison value and meaning. This is reactionary. The audience goes to the theatre to interrogate its own experience (that's its only possible function for people who shop in supermarkets, drive cars, build roads, change jobs, are told they need H-bombs, face street crime, etc. - not a life that can be calmed and explained by the sure change of seasons). Their experience makes them ask why? In our consumer society - where real responsibility is denied by pseudo-democracy people are relieved to be told that the answers are clear and need only be driven home by punitive violence relieved by a little sentimentality: the answer to starvation caused by militarism and agrochemicals is charity... The answer to crime is death - or even (in recent American films) lynch law mentality. It means we need a new aesthetics - a new way of directing and acting, which would be appropriate to the relations between east and west, the third world and the rich world. Our present theatre has manufactured the formula: beauty is lies and lies is beauty and that is all we need to know. A symptom of this barbarism (let's use the proper warning) is the National Theatre's artistic director's sliding of the

---

[4] This letter about the use of music in the RSC production of *Restoration* appears in Volume 2 of Edward Bond's letters to be published by Gordon and Breach.

words "spiritual revival" and "musical revival" - as if they were one. In America religion is now openly reactionary - and often openly fascistic (there are revivalist meetings in death row where condemned sing along with the idea of "Hallelujah, we're going to the Lord...").

I think that a great deal of modern aesthetics is actually a form of barbarism. I dont mean that rhetorically. I mean that it sets vicious patterns for the mind: partly by proposing vicious ideas - and by being itself an exercise in viciousness. By that I mean, proposing answers to problems which support the self-exploiting, destructive society.

Yours sincerely,

Edward Bond

John Clemo

London, NW9   9 March 1990

Dear John Clemo,

       Thanks for your letter. Your comments on the Bush Jacket are very interesting.[1]

       I still found it difficult - in the time - to properly "found" the sequence that leads up to the doorbell. This sequence from the putting on of the dress to the doorbell, teaches the audience how to read the play. It has to be justified by naturalism, but what is really happening is the dramatization of the analysis. Its this which should always be the main object of dramatization. But if it escapes from realism it becomes isolated - cut off from the audience's life, something external. At the worst this becomes the sort of abstraction in horror movies, where we use devils and monsters to do the work of the kings and queens of ancient drama: to act our lives for us. But if the naturalism itself becomes the object of drama, then there is no analysis. I find this problem in Chekhov, from whom I learned much. He uses TEs just as I do - but they are not analytical. It's as if they turned naturalism inside out, gave out a special significance... but somehow lost all meaning. Chekhov is a founding father of the theatre of the absurd (not that he is destructive and opportunistic as most absurdist dramatists). His TEs (the snap in the air in *The Cherry Orchard*, the top, the little tunes, etc.) point to a significance which escapes the characters: they are like Moscow for the 3Ss [three sisters], an emptiness. Watching the 3ss [*Three Sisters*] reacting to Moscow we use the emptiness - we see that they are deluding themselves and so we are not seduced by emptiness/Moscow. But many of Chekhov's TEs in fact seduce Chekhov. He finds in them his own Moscow - his own significance outside analysis.

       The line is difficult to draw for a dramatist. But you have to draw it right. If you get it wrong you lie. Art always does depend on an element of lies - because it is, in one aspect, facing the future, almost in the future, yet it is positivist about the future - has to be, that's the utopian element in art. But how can you be - since the future is still unmade? Chekhov's humming top is really like Lucky's gabble: a denial of meaning appearing as meaningful. Except that

---

[1] Bond is referring to the London production of *Jackets II* which opened at the Bush Theatre on 27 February, 1990.

Beckett can be deliberately ironic about it. The problem of theatre is this: the tension between representation and analysis. You represent so as to identify. You find the meaning in the analysis. Hamlet's verse is a TE (W[illiam] S[hakespeare]'s blank verse is always TE): it is immensely artificial but is needed by WS to tell the plain truth. It should be an instrument of precision, and Hamlet himself goes so far as to say how his text should be acted. But again in WS, the untruth invades the real: the ghosts, the feudal ideology, the pretence that the grave diggers will always stand on firm earth so that Hamlet may be free to explore heaven and hell.

In *In The Company of Men* - which concerns the Hamlet problem - I've dropped Gertrude (except in a recite) and the ghost - the ghost appears farcically in the disappearing/reappearing body.[2] There is no world of meaning lying beyond the TEs which can somehow give the naturalism a meaning: no ghosts, no humming tops, no gabble. And so there is no longer any meaninglessness to dramatize. We have to dramatize what is strictly meaningful. When we do this we can return an intense theatricality to theatre. But it doesn't become the flatulence of happenings or the unutterably mysterious or the rarified world of art that can only be conveyed by the elite to elite. That is merely the humming top playing the screams and groans of Auschwitz: fake theatre.

I think this means that it's possible and necessary to melodramatize the analysis. But there are dangers in this. And of course it's its own form of lying. You can only take bits of naturalism, reposition them, heighten them (either with unnaturally more or unnaturally less energy): and so you are then distorting naturalism and meaning may then be fed back into events the wrong ways, as it were. In fact this now happens in late method acting: where passion is meant to justify itself. Passion in *Hamlet* leads to language: in late method acting if it led to language it would be embarrassing, the fake would become immediately obvious. That's why Arthur Miller must now write (since he avoids analysis) a sentimental, slack prose. So we must be careful that analytical TEs don't merely become heightened forms of naturalism. Especially so because in real life this kind of thing can happen. In real life people often seem to cross the barrier between being there (naturalism) and representing themselves there: as if they sent a delegate into hell or heaven to be different. When this happens I think it shows how unnatural their natural life is - how bogus, ideology-ridden, false,

---

2 "In the Company of Men" appears in *Two Post-Modern Plays*, London: Methuen, 1990.

evasive it is. But then we have seen a unity between reality and theatre: and we see one of the reasons why people need theatre - that in their natural life they are actors and that they go to the theatre to escape from acting and enter reality (that is the reality within fiction, why we need fictions: but which must always carry with them the risk of falsehoods). Any important language carries that risk. Mathematics can make errors - but not tell lies. Mathematics are therefore not creative, since the errors can be found out and corrected by the same methods which made the errors. This isn't true of language - ideology can't unveil itself - and poetry is always immediately false: we're not like clouds and birds and seas and trains. Yet we can use that sort of poetic language to make the future possible (mathematics remains locked in its cell). That is a basic problem in all art: what governs, directs the choice? In *Clockwork Orange*, you see a play which venerates evil and the obscure because that seems to be necessary to human possibility (the potential of lying).[3] Yet when you refer that back to society you see the play is based on objective lies - aversion therapy: the danger in the short sharp shock which is part of the long aching trivializing pain of capitalism. The deviants in the play are not working class, and their cult-language isn't working class: it's middle class, and really the play presents the hysterias of the public school dormitory.

So we find the guide to poetry and drama by reference to the street. We analyze the political situation objectively. There is no mysterious arcane poetic world of higher truth that is unapparent in the supermarket or the car wash or the law court. When we have an analysis of society then we know how to use the TEs of drama. This gives us not merely the targets for TEs - which units of the play to TE: which line, which sequence, gesture - it gives us the degree of TEing: moderation or excess - which would be useful to presenting the analysis, what would be the objective truth and its best possible aesthetic form.

This is a prelude to your suggestion that the Cell Scene in *J2* could be heightened - literally a matter of pulling hair, clutching at heads. Since you saw the play NP and I have reworked the scene.[4] It was important to stress that after the first series of laughs - at the moment of "I'm sorry:" that the woman addresses the corpse - that she tries to speak to the corpse. That is a complex idea. Who

---

[3] A *Clockwork Orange* was presented by the Royal Shakespeare Company and opened at the Barbican Centre, London on 6 February, 1990.

[4] Nick Philippou directed *Jackets II* in both Leicester (Haymarket, 1989) and London (Bush Theatre, 1990) with Bond assisting on both occasions.

tries to speak to a corpse - isn't that as bad as letting Hamlet have his ghost? But
don't we use the moment to show how people always try - must try - to cross
unbridgeable chasms because the hiatuses in their own lives are too wide to cross
- that they are damned by their politics, by the necessity of living - when (having
failed to recognize someone she knows intimately) she needs to address him as
"anyone" - because he matters? Why carry such courtesy into madness: aren't the
mad afraid of death - of horror films - why be courteous? We can show the gap
between the lies and truth - what the woman needs to establish for her humanity,
her sense of responsibility: she didn't recognize one particular person - but she
needs to recognize everyone. So the problem (acting problem) becomes how to
approach the corpse, how to touch it, how to try to ask its forgiveness - and then
how to laugh in its dead face: that the lie is something for which she lives - the
total love for her son in disregard for others. This is said to be a biological truth.
Yet it seems to me the Palermo Improvisation points to something otherwise: that
there is a more complex social human structure.[5] And I'd add that even if there
were a biological imperative here, then social learning could be built on it and
developed from it - and that this wouldn't be a repression - since love has no
proper object: and that her madness self-shock can lead to knowledge. (I put this
loosely but I want to get on.) How this is acted then becomes a rehearsal room
problem: how do we best show the woman's trap - and that she goes mad only
because she understands that it is a trap? The writing doesn't decide this - and
shouldn't, since it has to be a contrivance between the actresses and the role.

But one can say definitely that there is no satisfactory *method* way of
acting the TE because it isn't a matter of character - that would be naturalism - but
of analysis. TEs are strictly analytical. That is their new access to aesthetics.
The woman must know the character through and through, but the playing can't
be reduced to that knowledge or even to using that knowledge and exploiting the
potential of the reified stage (that the stage dictates its own laws) - the stage
doesn't do this any more than piano keys designate music. Misunderstanding this,
method theatre tries to push the aesthetic onto naturalism. But once we can free
and use the analysis (and it will exist in a modern text - I mean in politics; not in
calendar - just as blank verse exists for WS: it's the only possible mode of

---

[5] The Palermo Improvisation was a series of improvisations Bond conducted at the University
of Palermo which gave rise to the *War Plays*. Further details are provided in the commentary
on *The War Plays*, London: Methuen, 1991. 247.

conveyance of true stage presence) then we can refer to the street: and make our choice. Again, not something arcane and elusive - but direct, full of lies ("is this a dagger I see before me?") and truth. The woman does not see who the man is. That is what is astonishing. When I saw the first public preview I realized that truth hadn't come across (for us not "is this a dagger I see before me?": but what I see before me is not my son and therefore doesn't exist). So the scene was merely that of a noisy woman. Rehearsing the scene would require much work on the unfinished sentences - there must be dozens of them! And these are not broken off in a form of inverted Lucky-loquacity: they articulate the moment of "not seeing." And in the scene she never does finish that sentence. She finishes one sentence when she apologises to the corpse - but she cannot finish the new sentence (I now know that I did not see) when she tries to apologise to the mother.

Lest I'm accused of arrogance, I should say I didn't write the scene - merely recorded it: it comes out of the Palermo Improvisation - and is one of those moments when people cease acting and become themselves and why they go to the theatre to escape from acting. I know that's paradoxical, but it's true. Unfortunately, it means - since people then have to step out of the securities of naturalism - that they can be lied to - and this is often welcome (because, among other reasons, when they were kids they could only be addressed in forms of lies). It's a problem that, of course, I would like to work on. As it is, given the circumstances, we did our best. As our society needs lies, it will spend more time and energy manufacturing the falsehoods of *Clockwork Orange.*

About the Parson. The scenes are meant to be funny. I think it would be possible to act them as such. If *J1* and *J2* are played together, the Parson scenes take on a different structure. Actually, I shouldn't refer to *J1* and 2 - the play is a unity, not a double bill. We need to understand our community in history and among other cultures. Modern technology has made this not merely a psychological, institutional fact - it's made it a matter of gross geography. Races, cultures and machines mix now on our streets as well as in our minds: so the mind has that many fewer fictions to escape into. (Islamic children can't wear headscarves: why not? - because in our culture we believe in putting children into little uniforms which are versions of military tunics, even convict garb.) In the present production, the Parson scenes are not funny. The part needs to be moved further into TE. At one stage, it was played much more farcically - this is the actor's natural talent, I think. I objected to this because I thought it made the politics too easy. But we haven't put anything in its place. Clowns are always weak, aren't they? They're always just escaping danger. Suppose a puppeteer were the clown and the puppet a, say, tragic figure? You can imagine Chaplin getting into indescribable contortions with the puppet's strings - then what would the camera show: if it showed the puppet being bashed terribly against the sides of the puppet stage, coming undone, unbolted, splintering, losing its costume...? And then you showed Chaplin more and more entangled? What would you have shown? It would be terribly funny because the puppet and Chaplin would be in the same world - no ethereal resonance, just political fact. Suppose however that almost magically the puppet could remain merely slumped under the great hurricane of strings over its head - slumped say in the pose of a ruminating Hamlet? Then it would be heart-breaking because the puppet and Chaplin would be in different worlds. Chaplin would be damned. But later as Chaplin lay on the ground - chewing at the strings as he remembered that he was always hungry - the puppet would lie slumped and inert at one side of the theatre box - a dead puppet. Then I think the puppet and Chaplin would again be in the same world: and clearly it's near to tragic. Now instead of strings - think of lines: the words of the Parson scene. One needs to define three elements: puppet-strings-parson. I don't mean the officer is the puppet - all three elements are part of the parson. (About the officer: he does describe himself more or less as a puppet - but he's like a glove-puppet, there are no strings - he is a zombie: less of a problem.) What the playing of the parson needs is the ability to rapidly change from one character to another. This is the essence of the humour because the comedian presents a mask and there's a face behind it. This is true of the unflickering, untwitching Keaton: the body will suddenly move away from the face-mask and show that it lives its own life. It's the combination of brutality and finesse. What the performance lacks is pleasure: I don't think, at the moment, that the parson would eat the strings. The actor worked terribly hard at the part and is able to make so much of it work - but in the end it is not yet his part. I say that sadly. I don't mind it personally. But I would have liked the scene to work for him. It doesn't matter - he brings other things to it. But to say: I want you to be shot here - or here - or here - is to try to sort out the strings. Also, the audience won't give him the part: because they are afraid. Again, a lot could be done in rehearsal - because we know what we want. David Ryall said to me recently: you can't play one of your characters without coming to terms with something in yourself, challenging it, sacrificing it, recreating it.[6] This of a writer who plays down psychology? I don't - it's merely that I don't see it as an end - or as existing in itself.

Yours sincerely,

Edward Bond

---

6 These remarks were made by David Ryall to Edward Bond at a recording of *The Fool,* BBC Radio, 21 February, 1990.

John Clemo
London, NW9   24 June 1990

Dear John Clemo,

I think that socialism cannot be defeated (unless our species changes radically and comes to a cultural standstill - or unless it destroys itself militarily or economically/technologically). This is because socialism is not merely a political philosophy and practice - but it is also embodied in people physically. In order to live in a technological society - to be comfortable in it - people have to think in certain ways. Of course they can misthink in the form of certain enthusiasms, obsessions, and fanaticism: (fascism, born-again Christianity, etc.) but these illusions have finally to pay a physical toll which is beyond them, and so societies constantly return not to a point of equilibrium but to the middle-point of a pendulum swing. There is then a possibility of the swing continuing either way - it tends to swing back along its half-arc into reaction. But it doesnt have to. Ultimately the body seeks a sane mind because the body harbours madness even less willingly than the mind does. So socialism is a form of thought that ultimately has a physical guarantee. We think of physical satisfactions as belonging to the senses - which we supply with economic goods. But I think there is something beyond this: the body sensually desires that its mind should be sane - desire not as a "sensation" but as a need. The body has a horror of uniforms. You wouldnt think this if you looked at history - because of the ideological distortions which are necessary if ownership is to sustain its always weakening grip. So it seems to me that in advanced socialism there will be a curious way in which the body looks at the mind: the distinction between mind and body will not be so tragic as it now is with the mind prostituting the body in order to support its illusions and the body seducing the mind to escape from its illusions. The ultimate guarantee of development towards socialism is that it's what the body demands of the mind and vice versa. That the body has no need for connecting to ideology - which is always an effort for it. The body cannot sink into illusions as easily as the mind. So it's as if the life would have a unity - not be spasms of pain and boredom discharged in hectic and negative entertainment. It's this further area of socialism which becomes more important to me. This is because technology has been able to solve some of the problems of capitalism by supplying a cornucopia of goods: and so to possess and enjoy has become an end in itself. It's this that I believe is ultimately not the "wish" of the body: the body needs to live analytically, as well as the mind. It needs to own its place not be owned by it. Curiously socialism is the only form of ownership which does not entail some form of madness: this is because it is at base the place owning the person and the person owning the place. There are no institutional means of creating the individual which are independent of the individual. So although the individual is - has to be - still a social product, the ideological distortions of ownership would not be institutionalised in the psyche. This sounds visionary - but really is only sensible. But the process is difficult: it's not like getting blood out of a stone but getting blood into it! (Christianity - which is a vision in madness - uses this pattern as the basis of miracles: they usually consist in putting something positive into something negative, but they do it in an ideological form.) The thing that makes this possible is that the mind has in some way to connect to its incorporation into society - has to interpret society to itself: and society cannot be fully in control of this process although it provides the mental means by which the process takes place. This is the area which political theatre has got to become more aware of. Otherwise capitalism can brush it off. It means a theatre practice along the lines of TEs - because this replicates the process of incorporation which the mind has learned in order to be able to learn, but it does it in such a way that the mind has to test and recreate its learning. And it means utilising the relationship between the individual - character - and the social. Political theatre has tended to discount this because it regards subjectivity as a bourgeois invention. (So was the spinning jenny - or it anticipated the bourgeoisie, anyway.) If that's what it was it still cant be discounted - it has to be developed. The familiar problem of socialist consciousness - but which must now be seen as very wide. Lang's film *Metropolis* showed working class people in drab uniforms and the rich in exotic dress. Now on the streets you see ordinary people in bright exotic clothing. This isnt merely consumer manipulation (though of course it is that). It means the mind is dramatising itself in new ways. The terrible vulgarity and brutality of Thatcherism isnt even a dramatic madness: it's a sort of neurotic minimalist compulsion under all the activity: it is the madman asking not to be let outside his straight jacket. This situation is full of potential for theatre.

Best wishes,

Edward Bond

Benjamin May

Lancaster   22 March 1992

Dear Benjamin May,

      I understand your frustration and anger about Trevor Griffiths' Gulf play - at least I think I do; I haven't seen the play except for a small TV excerpt - to me it seemed confused. I notice your poem is about the audience rather than the play. I should like to say clearly why some people become Tories and others radicals (i.e. socialists - "radical Tories" are not radicals but reactionaries). I mean what is the reason within the paradox, the foundation of the psyche? Obviously there is a social tendency: some of the rich are radicals, some of the poor reactionaries - but the biased tendency comes in the ownership of power and so the ability to form minds. The poor are less free to choose. It seems to me that the reactionary psyche is based on hate - which then licenses love, duty, honour, etc. (though it perhaps always associates them with cynicism and opportunism); the radical psyche is based on innocence, that is on creativity as a basis; creativity in the reactionary psyche is not basic, it's the way in which hatred adapts itself to the world. Reaction wears a mask - the radical face is bare and almost flayed.

      These remarks dont get to the root of the problem. It's one I need to define urgently and want to find time to do so. But even in this state it makes distinctions possible. I disagree with many radical people - but if basically they are creative - live the paradox - then they have my support or at least forbearance. The goodness of reactionaries, on the other hand, is in the end destructive: it is the Xenia/Marthe problem.[1] You need two ways of arguing: one with reactionaries, one with radicals. With radicals you have to be in the end encouraging, helping to make distinctions clear, aware that you're dealing with a "basis" and not the distortions built on it. If you dont do this you will become frustrated and even despairing. It is said we must be stronger than our enemies, unfortunately we must also often be stronger than our friends. Friendship should be the right to mutual tolerance: within that tolerance, the drama of life can be free to create its own dynamics - we can release it. Otherwise we play to our own weaknesses. We become like the man on a crutch who asks the crutch where he

---

[1] *Summer* by Edward Bond, *Bond Plays:Four*, London: Methuen, 1992.

should go. Regard the failures of friends as lessons - the occasion to learn. The failures of radicalism always cause great pain - but they lack the hideous, nihilistic brutality of the actions of reactionaries. The idea that the end justifies the means is wrong. The two cant be so conveniently distinguished. This is because all means bifurcate many times over - we cannot determine *an* end. Hate, bluster, and passion may often look very alike. The sane love details; the mad love conceptions. It's in details that ends and means become one - that is the only experience we can have of peace in this unformed world. This isnt to remove the battle lines from society to the psyche - it's merely that only in the psyche can we accept responsibility for our acts - and it's in the psyche that time first becomes tragic: later it becomes hideous in society, if we deny the tragic. The tragic sense is always based on love. The ancients occluded tragedy with fear. We have to revivify it with responsibility. Men and women are as impotent as if they were gods and goddesses: all we have to help us is our ability to dramatize, which changes us from victims to creators. That is why the most profound social and psychological truth is: drama for politics sake. I don't suppose that helps much. I need to learn to say it more clearly.

It's also difficult to say more about TEs than I have. Really, it's a question, now, of showing and experiencing. Stage-action has been captured by Stanislavskian acting or by happenings. Happenings can have a meaning. Just as the white face of the clown has a meaning. The white face is his prison. The clown (often tragic) shows us a miracle: that the man survives in his prison - the tragic is that he cant escape - he could only become a warden - and that would mean entering another prison. So he is shrewd and sensitive: the great *rage* belongs to the circus lions - and their rage is tamed - but the act of taming is always presented as a crisis - it could go wrong. Only the clown can do nothing except survive. The trainer fights lions (even if they're only drugged pussy cats): the clown fights ghosts. Cant the clown become the ring master? Not in a circus. The whiteness of the clown's face is really prison bars. So the circus is a myth of play corrupted by power: but play gives the psyche some freedom. But suicide could also be presented as freedom. Murder *always* is. Even happenings have meanings - but the meanings are parasitic. Happenings create nothing - they merely recapitulate. Really they're quite utilitarian - like the nails that hold a box together. They are so mundane that we notice them: we don't usually notice the nails in the box, we search the contents, often witlessly.

The aim of TEs is to restore meaning in drama - content in context. So we use the customary events - there are no others - but show new meanings in them by using them differently. Meaning will not be revealed by the play. We think we understand the meaning of *Lear* because of what Lear and the others say - we feel they emotionally express themselves in an understandable way, and so we understand them. They express the meaning from within. They are victims of events - but they express themselves over these events and this - together with sufficient armies - transcends events and transubstantiates them. It's this last that no longer works. We no longer have armies to carry out the missions of the soul. It's as if Lear upset a table and threw a tea-set on the floor. An army appears - throws away the broken bits: suffering in tragedy - but rights the table and resets the unbroken bits. A God only has armies for servants. This does not work when the aim of art - to express the human spirit, as they would have said - is to democratise power so that we may be free. Here the metaphor of Lear and his armies breaks down - it would be misleading to follow it. We have to use all actions to show the nature of power within them. Who is aggressor, who is victim? Who is destroyed, who is created? The normal definitions will mislead. As we re-show an event (TE it), the audience re-experience it: the crisis of the circus (not Brechtian reflection: Brecht likes to pretend that watching a boxing match makes us all philosophers - but we confront the audience with blows *and* ideas) - and so the event becomes different for them (or, if they intend it to remain the same *they* have to become different: if things seem to remain the same that is because we have changed so as to enable them to be the same - not changed ourselves *and* them). I'm sorry if this sounds complicated: but how else can I formulate it? TEs are like juggling with events and things so that we can see what they are - juggling with them is the only way we have of making them stand still: we take their movement on ourselves, we are forced to take on the role of the world so that we can see what is really happening. We put ourselves in movement. When we are in a train that begins to move, the landscape seems to move, not us. In the TE, we move so that we can see the event/object as "still" - i.e. inspect it. This sounds odd because I put it in physical terms (which is how the actor must act it and the audience receive it) but really I'm thinking of movement/stillness in mental terms, in ideological readings, in emotional sets - all of the audience.

But I think, even in description, it's clear enough. In the area of TEs we can put a new meaning. Partly this will come from the expression of the characters - and to that extent, of the actors identification with them. Like Lear, they express what they feel. [But remember that feelings are the expression of ideas: Lear thinks he is a pitiful, abused King and expresses what being this feels like - we hear it in the language. Language is evocative and descriptive: Mother feeding infant, "Eat! -so that you may live!" - (evocative: "I want you to live.") - "dont do that with the spoon" -(open containers turned upside down lose their contents - descriptive). The infant learns the evocative and descriptive on his own body: the first words are ideas but also physical exercises. The tongue must be taught as much as the circus lion.] It would be pointless to deny this, that actors identify with characters: it's how the audience *hears* whatever way we choose to *speak*. So the actor expresses an emotion. But we should discriminate about the choice of emotion. The definition - the idea - wont be found within the psyche as in Stanislavsky. There is no normal expression of an idea. Plays usually hold opinions as to right and wrong, who is good and who bad. And good plays (*King Lear*, *Hamlet*, *Oedipus*) always deconstruct themselves - whatever they do with the pieces at the end. But we should be more creative about the choices of emotions we act: find them in the idea - not in the character's self or the actor's self. Lear owned his audience's ideas - that's what monarchy did in Jacobean times. He cheats terribly by even invading their private emotions: as a King, he has no right to - but he claims to be the most humble and destitute of his own subjects. So power is aligned with the personal. This reverses the medieval farce in which a boy became bishop, a fool became (for a day) a king. Lear enables the audience to humanize itself - but at the cost of political lies: for the space of the play he credits the audience with kingliness. That is the hidden TE - which we would have to re-TE into new actions. Where the Stanislavskian actor might think: "here I feel and produce joy," we might say: "No - rage." But we neednt - we could direct the action so that the audience see this joy is evil. But Lear's audience saw him as not always a poor tramp but sometimes a tyrant (but W[illiam] S[hakespeare] blurs the proper psychological development: just before he dies, Lear boasts of killing someone who might, in fact, have been very like the servant of Gloucester who was blinded). So we have re-read experience radically. What is Lear's joy when he boasts of killing a soldier? WS always gropes toward the truth but sometimes misses it: he, like Gloucester, is also blind. Does this mean that we can, after all, act as WS wanted Lear to be acted? No, because we dont have an army to pick up the pieces and rearrange them - or accept Lear's joy in killing a servant. (And from these actions we have to read a certain projection of the world). Obviously our play will tell a different sort of story - and so must be acted differently: "Lear is dead, long live the slave." Lear's army is the creation of his soul: the social and the soul are one in Lear. And still remain one for our audience. WS lived between two revolutions (one from above and one from the middle - and interestingly his plays fit an audience from the lower classes to fit into the needs of the owners of both the revolutions). So the connection between idea and emotion is disturbed: this disturbance is virtually the record of history as it describes the changing technologies. In fact, most of the audience will have mixed emotions and confused ideas - that's our time: God does not speak and we have not yet learned to be human - it is merely an ambition. The confusion has made happenings possible.

I must begin to end this letter. Instead of finding meaning within, the actor has always to express: why did I become an actor. After *Olly's Prison* one of the actors said: "That was the sort of work I wanted to do when I started to act - but had forgotten."[2] I hear this quite often. I dont want missionaries. But I think that actors don't become actors merely to show off or flaunt ego. Roughly, Stanislavskian actors gesture outwards - empowered by what they find within (the idea of themselves). But really all their gestures (and often the most extrovert) are of course pointing at themselves - the line of expression is outwards, but the dynamic is inwards. Hence, either the lack of focus - or the artificiality of focus. The lack of precision - the directions (given to the audience) are vague. The actor needs, instead, to point outwards: the energy comes from within but not the idea - he is pointing to the idea outside - his reading (philosophy) of the world. Meaning is not inscribed on the soul - it exists in society. So not merely does this require the actor to see his character in a new light: but also to perform differently. This is the crux of your letter - and the answers should be demonstrated rather than written about. Roughly, create a barrier between the immediate psyche and the act. The barrier is crossed by the actor's need to act (not the character's need to be itself). This changes the action and therefore what the actor is required to experience in order to do it. In *Olly's Prison* there is the following scene. Mike cuts down the hanged man - he cries (the crying is shown in a triangle of rope) - then he is seen stalking silently through a crowd - then he is seen gasping like someone who's run round the world (or like someone hanging, of course) - then he crawls under the bed and he is heard to sob: five (or so) sobs on a downward scale - the actor not seen, only the empty cell. In

---

2 Bond attended rehearsals for the filming of *Olly's Prison* at the British Broadcasting Company in December 1991.

performance, the actor cried drastically throughout... because the character was upset, and Stanislavsky said he must reproduce his turmoil etc, and we are all suffering people, etc. Then why does he hide under the bed? Why does he stalk silently in public? Why the rope triangle? - and then you can look at the other incidents of crying, mourning, grinning, laughing in the play. And then you can say what is the meaning of Lear's joy? The actor might say "I must cry - Im moved." So rehearse "To Be or Not to Be" while you clean your teeth. Or let Chico Mendes talk while he performs the actions of a rubber-tapper - or while he mends the hinges on the door through which he will come to be shot (TEs need more poetry, not less). Actually, when an actor brushes his teeth by the graveside it can be moving - the objective isnt to belittle the action (you do that when you romantically invent art by a pose and a funny voice) but to enhance its meaning, make it more powerful. The actor must be denied exhibitionism and prevented from collapsing into his self. The latter is based on fear and the former on impotence and anger.

Act the image - or the multiple image (action). Which will be found in the text or the relation of the text to society and people. Why does Mike stalk silently through the crowd - and can sob (not cry) only in his cell-chamber? In the same play, Ellen puts four lumps of sugar into a teacup and talks of hate. When I came to rehearsals, this was done as if it had no significance. I wanted to almost build the scene round it (think of the cup in the first scene). I've now given the scene a title (after the sugar lumps). I think an actress can feel this - the lumps of sugar in her fingers as a stroke of hate, the plop of their hitting the water, etc: I want to domesticate this passion so that it can become gigantic (heroic?) again.

I'll suggest how to TE a scene from *Troilus and Cressida*.[3] Cassandra screams (off) during the war council. It's a harrowing scream. Our nerves are on edge. The war counsellors react various ways. But consider. They know her screaming very well. They'd hear it a long way off. They begin to react before we, the spectators, hear it. Why have these soldiers stopped talking? Why are they turning aside - one "screwing up" - one sitting back in fear - one bored? Have they seen a vision of the battle-dead in their maps? Now (I notice), one is trembling with rage; why does one leave the table? When Cassandra enters she is

---

[3] Bond worked with Cicely Berry and the Royal Shakespeare Company in November/December, 1992 in Stratford-upon-Avon on scenes from Shakespeare's *Troilus and Cressida*, *King Lear* and his own play *Jackets*.

like music bringing sound to dumb instruments - we knew them before they seduced us with their tune. Her scream might even be a murmur. But why does she come from outside - perhaps she's been hiding under the table under the death-maps? She comes out from under it (as children do), and perhaps now her scream is a child's sob - like Hector's doomed son, like any doomed child? Perhaps she shows her sobbing face to these candidates for learning? Perhaps one takes out his bayonet and whittles at a piece of wood. Now it is the men who are screaming and not Cassandra. I dont know... you can think of the analysis yourself. But it becomes more dramatic - because it's more telling and less seductive - than the diva-scream. Field Marshall Haigh cried when - after the end of the first world war - he saw the battlefields for the first time. That's a TE (I got the idea of TEs from life - not the theatre) - but we need to go further. Do the tears show that he was really a sensitive, suffering human being merely doing his duty for civilization? That is the message of the Haigh Memorial Halls. Let us, rather, say he is crying because his tailor has ruined his uniform for the victory parade. Crude? But uniforms are desperately important to an army and so are victory parades: the uniform is a map of civilization. Perhaps we need to show him crying at both - and when he cries at his ruined uniform then he is most human because it's like a dog crying over his chain. (Lord R is wise when he dresses up for the hanging: Bob is being hanged for the sake of R's hat - because that hat is the uniform of the rule of law-and-order, as important as the hangman's drab). I hope these remarks are of some use.

What you are doing seems to show understanding of what I intended.

Regards,

Edward Bond

P.S. - The "un-TE'd" parts of the text (as it were) should often be used as preparation for the coming TE (or series of TE's) - like the runway and runway lights preparing for the approaching flight.

E.B.

Peter Smith

Leicester   28 December 1992

Dear Peter,

I've just held three weeks of actor workshops at Stratford RSC[1]. We worked on *Troilus and Cressida, Lear (King)*, and my *Jackets* - just a few scenes from each. I havent had much to do with Shakespeare since I wrote the *War Plays*. Being at the RSC brought it all back (as they say of vomit). The standard of work is catastrophic. "RSC" is a sort of aftershave they spray on everything. It must be good also for upholstery.

The plays - Shakespeare's or others - are not examined at all. They are made to work with an all purpose costume, wig, lighting rig, music (well actually two tunes: the big anthem and the "naughty-one") and even an emotion which comes with a volume control to increase the intensity. It all works together like a fly-blown orgy - the music, the lights, the costumes, the wigs all reach a climax together. But I suppose you've seen *Tamburlaine...*?

The workshops were interesting. Of course all the usual resistance even from those who were "committed." Why does Shakespeare remain interesting and useful? Its silly not to let students study *M[erchant] of V[enice]* - its a useful way to learn about racism. Tories may claim *T[roilus] and C[ressida]* as an expression of toryism. But the play itself is ruthless in its destruction of tory values. Structurally each scene of *T and C* is a rape - a "paradigm" is set up and then destroyed. Even the audience is raped - "I'll be dead in two months but I bequeath you my diseases." And war is shown as a maniac before the heroes attempt to glamorise it. Hector (the archetypal hero) compares himself - in his fourth line! - to a woman: at the end he changes the Trojan corrupter (Pandarus) for the more extreme corrupter (Thersites the Greek) - meets the perfect knight (unnamed - he kills him and strips him) - then strips himself and is gang-deathed by the Greeks... I've never met a critic who explains the perfect knight ideally armoured, and why the best (chivalry) and the worst (Thersites), encounter Hector before he strips for the ritual death. Structurally everything in the play is built round violation of people and values - with an insistence that is fanatic. Its this insistence that makes Shakespeare permanently useful. His plays remain

---

[1] Edward Bond and Cicely Berry held three weeks of workshops with nine RSC actors at The Other Place, Stratford-upon-Avon, 16 November - 4 December, 1992.

useful not because they enunciate values that last for all time but precisely because they do not. Structurally he combines and recombines the elements of his plays so that the central problem is exposed in all possible variations - its like a scientist examining every possibility in order to strip away illusions and pretences and expose what is really involved. *Lear* is about "the fall". God's favourite son was Satan till he fell and established hell. God invents a step-son (Christ) and sends him to earth to repeat Satan's rebellion - but in the form of submission. Christ is meant to be "perfect good" - actually when Christ was being crucified He looked sideways (to the left) and saw it was God hammering in the nails. Cordelia says I am Satan - perfect goodness. Lear says perfection must bend and be human: or Nothing will come of Nothing. The whole play turns on the idea of the fall. It begins with a joke about a good man falling into the wrong woman's lap. Gloucester falls from the cliff. To fall means a restraining bond has been broken. Cordelia is petrified of falling. Lear cuts his tightrope into three parts and still imagines he can walk without falling. Structurally all the scenes combine components of the text (which is why they're put in it) to go as far as possible without falling, till the breaking point is reached. Its because the components are chosen with audacity and honesty - nothing is left to chance or tradition - that the plays remain useful. But the meanings extracted from the confrontations change. The plays are very very badly written, the language is torturous in its combinations, relentless, hectic, over-written, and over-devised like the desperation of someone mad. As little as may be is left unexposed: Lear's madness gives him insight which condemns W[illiam] S[hakespeare's] final closure of the plot - just as does Hamlet's. Often WS can still depend somewhat on myth to reconcile the irreconcilable - but even that rarely is untested. This means, though, that the plays do not retain an historical meaning. They present enduring problems, the problems for which we have, as a species, devised imagination, which we then infest with reality. We have to believe we won the pools in order to live. Even when winning the pools is tragic... someone in *Olly's Prison* says of someone else: you'd cry even if you'd won the pools. Exactly. The Greeks said its better not to have been born but if that misfortune strikes you then its better to die soon. Then they said Hurray! - and went singing and dancing back to their city: because they have faced the problem and had had the strength to kill God before he could crucify them. (Of course they killed him too soon, before they had the right weapons to do it and the right tools to live without him - but humankind is impatient.) The structures always open up the problem because structures belong to problems and not solutions.

This is the reason for TE (which you may have read of in the intro to the *War Plays*). It's only possible to use the classics properly by TEing them. For instance we (in the workshops) TE'd the scene of Gloucester's blinding. Why isnt G[loucester] brought on bound? He has to be shown resisting. Binding G is a feudal offence - the equivalent mirror-image of L[ear] cutting his tightrope into three. So we acted resistance - of a feudal and servant sort. In the end its a woman who insists on G being bound more tightly. Cornwall seeks revenge (he says it) and this is a feudal offence (between members of the same ruling class). And then the servant intervenes. He's says I've served you since I was a child (that is, he identifies a life-role: doesnt merely say 20, 30 years) - and he tries to help Glouc. Normally this is staged as a gesture - but we TE'd the scene. If its difficult for servants to bind G at the start of the scene, it is very difficult for a servant to defy his Lord. How does the Lord react? If the rules are so drastically broken it would be difficult to react - so we let the servant unbind G - who now has one eye (the difficulty of breaking rules and making new ones). He's almost unbound before Cornwall can react. There is a fight - two other servants watch. G has toppled over in the chair - he crawls away. (Difficult to break rules). And then the servant is killed. Some texts say the woman stabs him in the back - in a flash the actors knew how to do this: I drop the sword, you run round there, I catch his attention, you... But I insist that rules are difficult to break and when they are the breakage is open. So she takes the sword from the servant: another rule is broken, women dont fight. And she stabs him from the front - with his own sword. And his hand remains open and undefending, because another rule is broken - by the woman, who kills. (The decision to blind Gloucester is also made by a woman - in a brilliant one liner. She says it and goes: it is difficult etc.) The rules are broken - Gloucester blinded, Cornwall wounded, L's daughter irretrievably committed to evil - the servant dead. When Cornwall and his wife leave the servants do not go immediately to Gloucester - instead they go to the dead servant. Is he really dead? - and while they take care of the dead servant they also consider what to do with G. I was first told (in the workshops) that the flax and egg image was something that only the women in the group could really understand because it had to do with cooking. Yet men use it?... Flax are ropes and WS combines them with the egg of birth. He combines the grave with birth and who knows (at this stage of the play) if its a coffin or a cradle? Beckett would say that the child is tugged from the womb with the hangman's rope round his neck. WS has a further problem: the body hanging on the rope and suffering death will not die but will go on talking. And so the play recombines its elements in order to go on exploring how goodness is allowed into God's world - and if there is no God what goes on in his place? In the end WS provides a feudal-pro-capitalist answer - always unsatisfactory, because then he is applying an interpretation as a value: need is being replaced by want. But we can TE the scene to bring out the importance of the servant's act - and the collapse of the value (not nicely and neatly killing the servant by director's subterfuge from behind: but brazenly from the front). The elements are there for us to use. We see in the scene a meaning that WS did not - but which the structure allows. A less scrupulous dramatist would not have allowed the servant to intervene, he would have kept to all the rules, social and dramatic. All WS's best lines follow cracks in the old world. At the end just before he dies Lear boasts of just having killed a loyal servant (the hangman, doing a good state-job even if the circumstances require him to do it surreptitiously). (There's a lot more to this hanging - try staging it. It couldn't have happened as the officer [in another one-liner] confirms it did.) Perhaps Lear should come on with the bloodied sword - like the one used in the blinding scene. Let us take him at his word! He boasts of being a killer - and praises someone else for being one. L just isnt a serene saint. Or he could come on with the rope. The scene is pantomime, incredibly badly written: first she's dead, then she isnt, then she is - O yes she is, O no she isnt etc. Half way through this great scene the others on stage ignore Lear (while they divide up power and the kingdom again) till someone says "O look O look!" The text doesnt say at what. WS probably meant he should still be mooning over Cordelia (I have to say: the first syllable in her name is rope) as a noble dying King should. But the text is too honest. He's just accused his friends of murdering her - not in a passing flush of anger but a storm-like accusation - we TE'd it by having Lear beat them with the hanging rope. So what does he do while they divide the kingdom again? I took a clue from G's blinding. The moment he loses his second eye he seems - not at all to yelp with pain (thats sketched in with the loss of the first eye, the first step of the fall) - instead he has a conversation with someone who isnt there, his "good" son. Quite a rational, purposeful conversation. As you might after falling, he's entered into a world with a logic of his own. The conversation with an invisible person is natural in his world: the RSC multi-purpose emotion doesnt begin to reach it because it isnt a matter of volume and intensity but of the actor understanding the situation. So L picks up his rope and in his lunacy bowing, scraping, smiling and weeping showed the invisible spectators - perhaps the subjects he was once responsible for - the cut end of the rope, the evidence that he solved it all. He even dies in illusion, believing that Cord is alive: though long ago she had insisted that he cut her throat so that she might be immaculate. And so on. So we can TE the scene - and the play - for our own time. Actually, the whole cycle of Shakespeare's plays is an anti-poem: but this can only be understood when we realise that all good poetry is anti-poetry and either desperate or precise, as appropriate.

I think the theatrical technique of TE allows us to use WS for our own time. It means, incidentally, that the actors must always base their work not on Stanislavskian soul-searching (recollection-hunting) but on their imaginative experience. This is essential: imagination is always *need* and in the end its what prevents us being corrupted by *want*. Imagination always reproduces the problem. But thats another question and I cant go into it here.

I dont know if these comments will help you.

Yours sincerely,

Edward Bond

Chapter Three

Politics

Ria Julian
Kaposvar
Rakoczi, Hungary   26 January 1988

Dear Ria,

Thanks for your letter. The conditions under which you're working seem ideal. How can you best use them? Obviously by being of use to your audience. But in such a situation, where you have your working facilities and the support of intelligent friends, you can do more. Perhaps you have left the golden mountain for the golden city? You should try to find out what acting means. Animals only pretend to be in another state than they really are, when they're in extreme danger. A fox plays dead when it's trapped, some birds pretend to be lame when their young are in danger. The chameleon changes its colour - as if it said yes to whatever its enemy said. Yet acting we so often associate with the frivolous and incidental. Yet to me it seems, like laughing, a sign of the human. If humans didnt laugh they couldnt imagine heaven or build hell: laughing places a great distance between the knower and the known, yet enables the knower to keep a grasp on what he knows (the physical equivalent of laughing is an arm ten miles long). We laugh at what we dont know - and so the laugh is always secret: really the joke is our enemy because he always asks more of us than we want to give: in *that* he is like the saints, only without their self-humiliation. The clown teaches us that all the things we hold onto to protect ourselves become our burdens.

It seems to me that acting cant be frivolous. Rightly understood we act when we are in extreme danger. It's when we can no longer grasp the things that are in our hands. Hamlet has ghosts, sentries, and the company of actors: and each belongs to the others. Hamlet is sentry at the play - and tells his friends to keep watch. The actors are commandable ghosts. And the ghost is an actor with a real knife, real blood - and makes real corpses. Acting is always on the borders of our existence: I think we acted even before we began to build with stones. I've heard somewhere that civilization became possible when humans understood the lie - that they could elaborately deceive, scheme, contrive - and to take by cunning what wasnt theirs. And after all, a lie may defend one against corrupt power. And yet civilization is always a flight from its own tools - and I say this as a Marxist. The liars become interested in truth because they cant understand their own lies - just as we cant understand the inside of the joke. Acting is a search for the truth, which appears in the form (of course) of a lie or a falsity. We *play* because that is our first defence against bullets, bombs, waste, social diseases - not our only defence, but the first, and the one we retreat to. I believe the starving exist in delirium - and so do the affluent, who live at the expense of others: they are condemned to accept the lie as truth - and that is when ideology becomes corrupting. The laugh must have its secret, and the clown must be dangerous: but military killings - when they enforce lies - become banal and kitschy - "they" kill because they have nothing to die for. Delirium is of course a disease of the imagination. Imagination has one superiority over facts, it gives them their meaning: death is a fact but what gives it its meaning? Well, how did it occur - in what cause, through what neglect, to what point? These questions cant be answered without imagination. The church founded its bookish theology on a drama - a version of the Oedipus story as cunning in its own way as Shakespeare's Hamlet version. Eating makes all people like children, to eat is to be a child, to relate to things as a child does, to sit and be given; imagination is somewhat stronger - it ingests (as food) but its projections are mental, and so it's as if the child created the world - that is the nature of imagination. I dont hold any truck with the cult of the child - we only envy the child because we're so stupid. But imagination gives us all the potency of the child, the child's sense of responsibility - and yet gives us, or can give us, the strength of giants. Any human being who really understands the child becomes a giant. That is the task of the actor - and of the playwright. It can give us the strength to deal with bullets and bombs.

You ask which of my plays to do. Fortunately I dont have to decide. Depends on what's most useful to you at the moment. The *War Plays* are the best things I've written - they touch on some of the foundation blocks of dramatic method, and those blocks, carved in stone by the Greeks, and set in religious faith by primitive peoples, must move whenever they're touched. But the plays are hard to do - there is no existing dramatic method for them, no time for the actor to disarm himself before them, no reason (therefore) to do them. But perhaps in your theatre it would be possible?

Now I have to deal with Thatcher, since you repeatedly ask. The most significant thing about Thatcher is her extreme ordinariness. The great strength of the English was their ordinariness - anything more testing they hived off as eccentricity. Ordinariness makes it possible to take away everything that matters while appearing to give - at least in peace time. Twenty years ago the Labour party was talking about the white heat of technology. Thatcher has taken power over technology just when its expotential rate of development has taken off. For any unit of labour invested in material things in the past to produce a product of 10, a product of 100 can now be produced (the technology of the H bomb is less complex than that of a coal-fired power station). Cheap sources of labour are still needed - it doesnt seem possible for capitalism to produce money surpluses without extracting labour power: though money may be made incremental on itself, without touching any physical goods. This is Thatcher's second great opportunity: she came to power when new sources of financing were being invented. The New York Stock Exchange had been deregulated in the seventies. This created a fight for custom, and this was fiercely fuelled by the new technologies of information: deals could be made in fractions of the time previously necessary - the clock speeded up. Modern technology was exported to the East - the new source of cheap labour. Financial artifacts like junk bonds and Eurodollars were created. So Thatcherism latched into world developments. At home, by selling off public industries and property, she created seed investment money. So technology gave flesh to the ghost in various ways: it became possible for people to make their dreams solid. Even those without could imagine that soon they would be with. However, the misuse of reason always creates violence: so Thatcher is synonymous with bombs, war, capital punishment, city brutality: whatever we do in fact, we pay for in imagination - the imaginary extends the real and puts it in its context, and thus has the strength of the real: as much as we change our landscapes, we change ourselves - we *must* be wounded by the knife in our pocket. That isnt a philosophy of quietism, because that would submit us to Thatcherism and more extreme forms of fascism. It merely records the human condition: the good dreams cost as much as the bad, but we must have the good dreams or the bad dreams will certainly destroy us.

A beast moving in the dark always pushes its nose ahead of the rest of its body. A human beast moving in the dark always pushes its claws ahead: you can always tell any form of reaction, fascism, Thatcherism, whatever, by its claws - it is always a philosophy of violence with a retrogressive pattern of "human nature" -and since our imagination must become our reality (that's the peculiar characteristic of the machine-and-tool maker) people like Thatcher are very dangerous: they are ordinary. That also makes them virtuous - and better the anarchic reaction of a lumpenproletariate than the virtues of the middle-class, since cynicism is healthier than righteousness and less harmful to your neighbours.

You could always do *Human Cannon*. It appears to be a tragic play - but in performance it becomes strangely festive and exhilarating. I'd answer any question you had about it, though it's pretty straightforward.

Yours,

Edward Bond

Gulsen Sayin
Ankara, Turkey   23 March 1988

Dear Gulsen Sayin,

    Thanks for your letter. I'll try to answer your questions. You ask about the psychology of my plays. It's a question that greatly interests me. I think we inherit a culture and that this is the basis of our psychology. I dont think we inherit (if I can put it this way) our biology directly from nature: but from an encultured biology of our parents. I think the human psyche is "potential" rather than actual. That means, for example, that our instincts do not direct our way of life: they merely connect our body with our culture. We usually think of culture as an effort to adapt our animal nature to a human society. I dont think this is so. The human brain is vast in comparison with the brain of animals. This doesnt mean that it extends, exaggerates, the animal brain, so that its contents are merely enlarged: it creates a space, an openness - and the animal brain is lost in this, it vanishes in the new potential - like one footprint lost in a desert. We shouldnt think of the human brain as struggling to exist with the animal brain: we have a different sort of psyche - and its contents are social. These include the performance of physical (and to that extent animal) functions - but they place them in a space and with an awareness of time that radically alters them. The brain of the animal is too small for its animal needs. Our brains are infinitely larger than any simple evolutionary need - its capacity to speculate and invent requires the concept of future, and any society always half exists in the future. Our danger isnt our atavistic animal inheritance; instead we are endangered by the future, by the demands it places on us - we're constantly trying to fit history into the future - this is because human invention always brings the future into the present. That's why societies change.

    I have no personal interest in violence. Nor do I have any aesthetic interest in it - as perhaps Artaud does in the Theatre of Cruelty, using aesthetic means to shock an audience. Artaud had been subjected to electrical shocks in medical institutions and he should have known better. Nor do I use (as you ask) violence to create theatrical tension. I merely record it in order that it should be identified. Imagine an identity parade: someone has been assaulted, and they're shown a row of people - or better (for this example) a series of photographs: when the victim comes to a certain photograph he or she recognizes the assailant

and is shocked - it's the shock of recognition I'd like: it may happen that the
victim recognizes the assailant as himself or herself - this is also a useful shock.
It's sometimes said that the shock in theatre is counterproductive because it allows
or encourages the audience to "switch off." I dont think this happens - the victim
when he or she sees the photograph doesnt say: I am shocked and therefore I will
pretend that the crime, the incident, didnt take place. If I *merely* shocked this
might be possible - but I dont, as perhaps Artaud does.

I write (I was born) in an age of mass destruction inconceivable before.
And destruction of a different form. If I were a 16th century zealot and I burned
a heretic or witch, I'd've done so for partly aesthetic reasons: the Bible said I
should, and the Bible is an aesthetic work of art (as are all religious writings). If I
bomb a city or take part in a political extermination, it's because the "form" says
so - the government document, and it has no aesthetic context. So our deeds
become naked and brutal - they serve our own ends, not those of a god. At the
same time, just as religion admonishes its believers with hell and the day of
judgement, we can create hell and final solutions - the nuclear holocaust and so
on. All this means that the theatre is changed just as human psychology is
changed: it isnt that beliefs change, but that what it means to believe changes -
that the structures (which are social) in the mind change - we function differently.
Of course the relics of the past still clutter up the present - we're like starving
people who read a book on good table manners. So there is a hiatus in our psyche
- and this is the hiatus that art is meant to fill. Our species invented art - it isnt
the same aesthetics as the colouring of a bird: just as our legs arent the same as
the legs of a horse: we wear maps on our feet, the horse doesnt. So art always
fills a vacuum. The point is important because it means that art is invented - not
created in the usual sense, which is taken to mean a delving into something
aboriginal: the past begins with us, it's only the future that exists independently of
us. The response of art has therefore to be one of responding to a time of danger.
It seems to me that in the past sinners could look at pictures of the last judgement
with some security: they werent among the damned, or would try to live as if they
werent or would repent so that they would not be. You cant look at a picture of a
hydrogen bomb explosion in the same way. Of course no one says it - but the
basic premise of art now is our potential self-destruction: consumerism is merely
the wreathes on our future graves. Aesthetics can become consumerism: but then
it isnt art. Aesthetics has no access to any profundity. I conclude from that that
in the past it was possible to treat an audience in a certain way: you wrote on their

backs while they looked at the stage. They could then choose to read what was on their backs. This is true even of someone like Brecht. You can misinterpret *Mother Courage* (notoriously). Dreigroschenoper opera can be a "tarted up operetta" - the moon becomes a paper cut-out, the troops are Kiplingesque soldiers (in the cannon song) - not the Nazi troops being trained down the road. But now we have walked on the moon - or rather a soldier has; and the things about which Brecht warned us have come to pass. So I cant write on the audience's back anymore: I must confront them face to face. Of course I reassure and encourage then, but I use the theatre to approach them, not to stand between me and them. My plays are not violent. But I place violence in the plays. We think of aesthetics as being applied to the stage - in colour movement sound (music and effects) etc - but this isnt so: analysis exists on the stage, and it does so in its own right: because it is submerged in society (and the usual member of society knows no more about the structures of his or her life than a duck knows about evolution or the effect of the moon on the tides, and all the aesthetic splendour of its plumage wont bring it nearer to an understanding of them). So the analysis of life has to be placed on the stage. This cant be done schematically, and so there have to be "units of reality" in which certain things, moments or situations are *used* to explain: they arent directly explanatory as a diagram: the interpretation doesnt consist in the story, the story must be interpreted as it goes along, it must express its interpretation: the end cant give a meaning to the story. So it's the analysis that produces the aesthetic: and instead of thinking of the aesthetic as being applied to the audience: the audience is the arena of the aesthetic. If there has to be a prisoner in the theatre it should be the actors and not the audience: the actor can only create when he or she knows his or her cell. We must avoid aesthetics becoming consumerist - that would be the real, moral, theatre of cruelty.

So I wish to be grim to an audience? Is this question valid in the age of the disaster movie? I want an aesthetics that celebrates our humanity by using it - not by pointing at it. Most actors reduce themselves to chimps taking part in a tea party - but because they play kings and saints and use words like love, eternity, damnation, ambition, armies, they dont notice this: and even the suggestion is no doubt offensive. Yet Im sure that most of the audience at the National Theatre or the Royal Shakespeare would be much happier watching a chimpanzee bun-fight at the zoo. After all, the shock of creatures behaving like us, yet having no understanding of what they're doing as they poise the cup delicately above the

So what is the "serious theatre" to do? Stage *Lilac Time* in a concentration camp or an Ayckbourn play in Auschwitz? It would be better - aesthetics would begin to take on a discipline. The genuinely trivial and the genuinely serious have always succeeded in contrast. The trouble would be that it didnt approach the audience as a moral and political agent. That's what I try to do - and it's why I call my plays "rational theatre": the audience experience meaninglessness (or anger as a corrective to the meaningless behaviour of others) in their own lives and I try to give that meaning but in an aesthetic experience which is a practical exercise of meaning: (in the sense that you cant speak a language until you know the meaning of its grammar, though the grammar itself has no meaning and can only be described by the language it creates).

The theatre is a place of very strange truths - as you might suspect from such an ancient and spectacular institution, still closely replicating its origins. The churches have radically changed - theology constantly refashions the world. Armies have also largely changed. You couldnt seriously reproduce a 5th century Greek battle - or religious rite: you can do that with a Greek drama. And if you could go back a million years to earlier theatres (which there were) you could still use their plays: you could also still use their fires and saucepans and tables - you could still eat their food. Theatre is as close to life as these things: it's merely that it exists in a space in the head. Of course the meaning of theatre constantly changes - the meaning of *Antigone* isnt the same for us as it was for the Greeks: but it expresses precisely our need to understand a situation by describing certain constant elements in that situation and by emphatically stating our need for a solution - and the sufferings consequent on failure: which dont change, except in scale. What is theatre basically about? It is there to teach the audience how to act. The audience will of course never need to act, and may well never want to. But "acting" or "actuality" (does the pun only exist in English?) must be created in the space in the head - a new form of humanity for the future which confronts the audience, for the struggle in the present: that's the connection between the space of the stage and the space of the brain. The space-stage is limitless because you can artistically extend it to infinity - your fingernail can be the place of armies: the head is limitless because imagination has no boundary; speculation constantly encroaches on its ignorance, hoping that the extending boundary will reflect back onto the ignorance of the centre, from which the search for extension is propelled. So the audience (to go back to my question about grimness and disaster movies) is prepared to receive whatever will activate itself on that space -

and I suppose the intercourse between the boundary and the centre has already created certain concerns, enthusiasms, obsessions, needs and these become the subject of drama. I cant think of any reason why audiences should be attracted to tragedy and melodrama if this isnt so. Aristotle cant be right - if he were, the games of the Colosseum would be higher art than the plays of Sophocles and Euripides - they would certainly incite and purge to a greater extent. Then what advantage does the drama have over the games? - it has meaning. So on the stage you put the strenuous, the tragic, the dangerous - because they are part of the day in the brain, they are the events to take place in the space. The aesthetics of entertainment doesnt create in this space: it reproduces what the audience already recognizes. And that, quite strictly, means to turn the place of the stage into a place of prostitution. We all know that the great crime of consumerism is that the product consumes the consumer: we're eaten by the Coca-Cola can, the latest gadgets gnaw away at our cities, the newest fashion corrupts our institutions. If the world perishes it will be because we have corrupted the audience. The audience was the first assembly of civilization.

Democratic forms as we now have them enable the functioning of technology but they do not allow the humanization of our species: technology combined with modern democracy has more and more taken away people's responsibility for their own life. In the human psyche there is a desert, and we have to go into that empty desert because there we will make a meeting - that is the function of art, to arrange the meeting. When that happens, or we are certain we have begun that journey, we would accept responsibility for our societies, and the democratic forms would become real.

Finally you ask me if Im satisfied with the present productions of my plays. No.

Yours sincerely,

Edward Bond

Roberta Galeotti

Ferrara, Italy   16 December 1988

Dear Ms. Galeotti,

Thanks for your letter. Im sorry I wasnt able to meet you while you were in England. I will try to answer your questions.

1. What Brechtian elements have influenced my writing? To see the individual as a social subject. Subjective experience in the audience - and therefore the reduction of characters to subjective dimension - fail to solve social problems or to properly integrate the audience with society. This means turning away from questions concerning individual welfare - which are at best medical-psychological, and at worse spiritual when dealt with in theatre - to questions of the welfare of individuals in society.

2. Why do I show grotesque and extreme incidents in everyday life? I think the meaning of our lives - the problems which show up in political and economic forms - is symbolic: we interpret the world in terms of a mind which is many layered, so that questions have to appeal to both the infant and the philosopher in us: just as physically we're very much primary animals with basic needs as well as being capable of heroic form, great dancers, skilful acrobats and surgeons etc. I dont mean that our social problems are psychologically caused - because the real world has its own dynamics and necessities - partly we respond to these as physical objects (we die, we get disease, are well fed, etc) but partly we respond to it psychologically and this means that we also create it. Politics and the rest of our lives are the impact between total freedom and total necessity - I know this sounds contradictory, but it is in fact the substance of our lives. We create our fate and are then bound by it. But because of this it's always possible to recreate, change our fate - but we do so as prisoners who must struggle in various ways. I suppose we will only become human when we have stopped creating "fate" for ourselves, when human beings have stopped being one another's enemy, with all the political distortions this brings. Then we will of course still live subject to physical necessity but we will accept this in freedom, we will be free creators of ourselves. The individual will even then, though, be in conflict with herself or himself because of the way the mind is created through experience - but this is a humane dissatisfaction, and our society will not (then)

turn it into a curse. The causes which now make us devils (so often) will then make us into human gods. The grotesque and the extreme are these tensions having their psychological and political expression. I dont of course think that people are innately evil, and I think it is philosophically incoherent to say they are innately violent in the sense that they are, say, innately breathers.

3. Why are my plays, and their styles, experimental? I think that an aesthetic form no longer contains any truth - as say Greek architecture expressed, cogently, the social and extra-social relations of Greek society; or the art of the Renaissance did the same for the Italians. Not that these styles solved social problems by being full interpretations of human abilities to control. Michelangelo's architecture is partly based on the notions of weight, of stones crushing the ground, threatening people who enter the doors of his rooms. Yet it works for us in some ways like the soaring architecture of Gothic churches - in fact, it soars even more! This is because Gothic architecture fantasizes the stone and so the buildings seem empty. Believers find them filled with God of course. I find them filled with tears, with emptiness, with aspirations. By recognising the imprisoned nature of social men and women Michelangelo goes another step nearer to their liberation. If the political freedom of human beings depends on their social relations, and this in turn depends on their technological relations to their society, a process is carried out through tools and institutions of ownership - then in some sense that technology will show each period's art. We however are now so technologically powerful that we have erased the economic need for scarcity and want: these things still exist only for political and cultural reasons. But it follows from this that artistic "truth" (in the end, demonstrating social and natural relations) no longer has any "set" style. That seems to be the position of postmodernism, which did not exist when I began to write - but which I imagine like many other people I anticipated. But we cannot copy the art of the past because we cannot be agent of its necessity. I think there is a new situation for human beings. So now we produce (at least in quantity) more art than previous societies - but the truth which in the past, in art, was proposed by necessity is now a matter of choice. Of course, the choice is often solved financially (business as patrons etc.). In the past the final arbiter of communities was the physical, necessary world: now it is the cultural world, and so we have to create culture which expresses "human necessity" so that we may be free and not destroy ourselves. If God is not dead we shall not live - is another way of putting it.

(God is an image that collapses the natural world and the human world into one - and makes political control more skilful and imposing: that is, it contains both the good and the bad, but for bad reasons - and so religious people burned heretics for their own good etc.) The danger is that we make of politics a new god - which is what Stalinism was about. It tried to produce a human form of necessity - and this would allow us the crimes of the ancient gods (you will see that Stalin often behaved exactly like the God of the Old Testament) but we have to combine freedom with necessity (if we dont there is a psychological reaction,and people seem to reduce themselves to the passivity of things).

4. Why are some of my plays set in the past? I wrote a series of history plays dealing with the important turning points in history to try to understand what happened at these times. They become ideological patterns for us - and they're always a compromise between truth and lie, and we now have to expose the lie. Remember, that in human affairs the lie is always the foundation of truth: behind the political truth - the expression of humanity - there is always a lie, which is the means by which human beings were exploited (and by which the exploiters believed they were acting for the general good or at least according to necessity). I dont transfer our problems into the past. I show how the solutions of the past become part of our problems. But most of my plays are set in the present or the future - *Cannon*, *War Plays*, *Company Of Men*, *Jackets*, etc. to name some of the more recent.

5. You say the social attitudes of my plays dispose the audience to want to change society. What should they do? I am a Marxist socialist. I believe social power and social control must be common properties. This means abolishing privileges of education and welfare within society: it is bad to die of starvation but it is worse to die of starvation believing it is necessary to die of it. It is bad to go to a school reserved for poor people, but its worse to believe that you deserve, ought to go to such a school and that rich people are in some way more able to appreciate, get more from, a better education. And morally you could say whether you are rich or poor it is tragic to die of cancer but it is both tragic and immoral to die of it if you do so in a hospital where you - if you are rich - are made more comfortable than others with cancer who are poor. To accept social divisions means that you accept certain philosophical attitudes which are socially corrupting - and are themselves the cause of social diseases, such as violence, addiction, the war of the rich against the poor. To change this

state (which is our present one) you have to struggle in all situations - since the problem infects all situations. I think that modern societies need technological control centres, but that all affairs should also be dealt with at local levels - that there should be "groups" with political power at local levels. We shouldnt elect people to these groups - we should all have a right to debate in them and to vote. They would deal with all social and political problems, and the consensus would be transferred back to the higher levels. For instance, if the technological centre said that nuclear power stations were necessary, then locally it would be debated if the power station were to be situated in the local area. If everyone - all the localities - refused to have a nuclear power station - then it wouldnt be built. But the localities would know that they would have to manage without nuclear power. They would then have to accept full social responsibility for the final decision. Local decisions could become democratic "national" decisions. All aspects of society should be discussable and decidable in this way. We have to find ways of people being able to accept responsibilities for their lives. The "group" idea would mean that - once people had experience - local decisions would be made on national grounds - because people would see no conflict between national and local issues. They would accept responsibility for their society on a local level. This is only an example of democratic procedure. Democracy should be thought of as a biological tension of the human being - almost a physical freedom!

6.   You ask what are a playwright's fundamental problems?   The playwright deals with society and the individual. He shows characters living their lives. Any form of social rule has a doctrine as to the nature of the people it is ruling. People are such-and-such and therefore government has to be such-and-such. If social truth is always founded on a lie then the description of what human beings are will be false. Science will be falsely interpreted. We think of science as producing incorruptible truths which must be acknowledged. Outside of physical necessity this isnt so. The human mind becomes its belief about itself - as far as the higher (frontal lobe) functions are concerned - and it's these functions, after all, which give us our social and political problems. Otherwise we would be like other animals: faced only with the problems of necessity and endurance, not of necessity and freedom. The point is that acting and directing and play-making in general become involved in these difficulties. What we act is what we believe. So our acting is primitive because we interpret ourselves regressively. Acting tends to reduce characters to the packaging. We have to say

"why" has the writer put the characters on stage - not "who" are they because
we're dealing not with truths immediately - but with beliefs about beliefs. It's
only when the first belief is right that we could talk about political, moral, or
dramatic truth. Art isnt access to a social soul - pristine in its truth. Art is a
contrivance by which we create our humanity - images and patterns of it. I think
the theatre is still largely dominated by method acting - and the appropriate form
of playwriting. It is very easy to make things work on stage in socio-biological
terms - which is the philosophy behind the method (or treatment, I think it should
be called). We need to say "What shall we use this incident, scene, or character
for?" - and that means having an interpretation of society (which will become the
substance of the first belief). Beckett knows how his plays are to be acted -
because really he is dealing with and for the dead. (The dead's only sign of life is
that they laugh). I dont know how my scenes and characters should be acted - but
I know what they are about in that I know the problem they pose, or expose. If I
knew how they were to be acted I would have faked the problem. So like the
scientist we must always approach the work from a stance of scepticism.
Everything we have so far learned - and by knowing which we have passed our
exams - we must put in suspense - in *all* nonliteral senses of that word. And then
for that moment in the play - we invent a response of freedom and necessity.
That is the theatre work: the audience's work will be to respond to that moment or
event and this will be like learning very rapidly a new language. Of course we
always learn a new language by comparing it with our own - unless we're infants.
But the infant has created the problem of language for us - making it many-
faceted and giving it a concreteness through its ambivalence. Nevertheless, the
audience work should be like the moment when the new language begins to speak
to them on its own terms in its own grammar: a new synthesis - a new belief
about belief becoming fact because "it works." A thing is art only when the
street, the kitchen, the factory agree that it is. That is the total reality of the stage
- which is founded on its fiction. In art there are no white lies - all lies are mortal
in art. And this is true even though the truth of art - as in politics - is founded on
the temporary and transitory. Art cannot transcend human limitations. It is the
truth of action - rather than of some pristine, otherworldly fact. Beckett's plays
all take place on the seabed. They achieve profundity only because the people in
them are dead, drowned. Artists are like children, they have to take responsibility
for eternity. And they are like politicians, they have to take responsibility for the

day's prices in the shops. I hope these remarks will be of some use to you. You'll understand that I dont think a proper way of acting my plays has been produced - some are better than others.

Yours sincerely,

Edward Bond

Ahmed Elhag
London, SE22   4 April 1989

Dear Ahmed Elhag,

    About Postmodernism. We don't live in a postmodern world but in a
postmodern society. It means that style is no longer an indication of content.
Any writer needs to make contact with a public. If writers live in a postmodern
culture they have to use the elements of that culture. Otherwise the culture serves
as a barrier to communication. I don't think art can penetrate an ideology -
though it may sometimes move an ideology already in movement. But I think no
destructively dominant ideology can impose itself without in some way co-opting
progressive tendencies in society. Politicians appeal to the good not to the evil:
and when they denounce groups of people as evil they do so in the name of good.
The morally approvable has a public face, but this must also relate (in the general
mind) with private, directly experienced good. Of course even this latter is
socially formed and therefore politically structured - but it must meet very basic
human needs and it is (usually) a moral good that these needs are met. They're
not merely biological needs (such as food) but also psychological needs (such as
the experience of a developing psyche). But there is no unmoving point in
dialectics - there's no way in which thesis/antithesis can produce a superthesis
which creates it. This means, I think, that we're always being directed back to the
fundamental and the immediate. And isn't it there that ideology is often the
busiest? Even the concrete moves.
    Most postmodern practice is no doubt reactionary. But isn't much of its
aesthetics pointed to by Rimbaud? Yet who sees things more immediately than
Rimbaud? He sees a pair of hands as directly as Van Gogh sees a pair of shoes.
Van Gogh kills himself - Rimbaud abandons antibourgeois poetry and takes up
capitalist gun-running. Van Gogh shoots a hole in his head. Rimbaud fights with
a gun by the lake. Then he loses his leg. It's always as if the social distortions
come back as wounds on the poet's body. As if no difference could be made (in
the end) between the poet's image and the ideological representations. They both
come down to a shared reality - with which the poet/arms-dealer is struggling - or
surviving? We think of ideology as static and as imposing something on people.
Perhaps we should think of it as being more *directly* repressive - as enclosing
things within people so that they become distorted? Ideology doesn't provide

answers - it merely successfully asks questions. Of course public expression comes in the form of answers - "common sense," racism, etc.: but where did that superthesis come from? You can say "human nature." But to say that is reactionary. So we need to say that the subjective self - and the emotional psyche - are infiltrated by ideology: not in the sense that they are static and directly taught. It's more as if they "over-hear" the world, the language of the objective world. The subjective self is itself in contradiction. There are the contradictions of time - we live with our younger experiences and the way our younger needs were met and repeated. And there are the immediately objective contradictions of class-and-nationalist society: our taught relationship to society will not reflect but will distort our class experience within society. But both elements - the two contradictions - of this psyche will experience themselves in terms of social language, some of which is directly and the rest of which is often saturated with ideology. What would stop Rimbaud stopping the writing and taking up gun-running and dying of his leg wound? The gun-running and the leg wound are ideology creating objectivity. When are people silent? Christ before his accusers, Rimbaud before his business partners. Both have come to a moment when they are confounded by their own dynamic, their own searching. Both function (they are not mad) but neither can speak without accusing himself: Christ is silent because he is also Pilate the questioner. Rimbaud is silent because it has become a matter of money and therefore he is as silent as the corpse shot by the gun. What happens in these cases (and obviously I'm choosing two of the more spectacular) is that, because truth is so locked into ideology, ideology becomes destructive, terminal, when the search for truth (understanding, analysis, dialectical movement) is driven to its historical limit. The limit changes historically. Does this mean that even one's direct class knowledge is ideologically tampered with? I think that's true - because history is incomplete and therefore we compromise with the actual even when we propose the possible. So it's as if the search for the truth runs out of ideology. That's a historical limitation. Grammar remains constant but language changes. It's as if the more we can manipulate (scientific) objectivity the more the psyche can be substantiated by that objectivity; and by then returning - through action and inspection - to objectivity it can de-ideologise objectivity. But it's a reciprocal process. Our (potential, since it undulates with the economic climate) grasp on reality and control of ourselves in reality becomes historically greater: we are (in theory) spared the silence of Christ and the gun-running of Rimbaud. But then (to achieve this) you have to have cultural intervention in human subjectivity. I think art is an essential biological process for stabilizing the human brain: synthesizing it with changing reality (this doesn't mean that art partakes of the biological any more than lungs are made of air). But to do this you must use the ideological language of the social psyche - even over class fractures. There is no other language. But don't confuse the language with a grammar. That would be a reactionary form of Postmodernism. We can use ideology conflicts within the human psyche in order to make that psyche more objective, more continuous with the world of things (though not more thing-like). If you do anything less, ideology will rephrase it in the audience's mind.

I hope these remarks are of use to you. For me, they indicate the reasons why writing has become more interesting. Reactionary Postmodernism fluctuates between the grandiose and the cute. We can use Postmodernism to close the dangerous killing space between psychology and the world of things, between the ego and society, between the humanely responsible and the functional and organisational. Otherwise, we waste our lives and abuse the lives of the unborn - in fact, we ideologically exploit them if we refuse to address our own times in the common language. We can turn that language into a weapon.

I've got a play on at the Pit which you could see if you can afford it![1] (I hardly could! But you can only change one contradiction for another so you should confront the contradictions where you can be most effective.) The production isn't ideal, but it's better than it was. In a way, I'd regard that play (*Restoration*) as postmodern in that it shows that style is inherently contradictory and excludes in the act of including.

Best wishes,

Edward Bond

P.S.- I should add that I don't see cultural work as a substitute for other political work or for understanding class experience - but as a way of radicalising political work and making class experience politically effective. Art should be a source of

---

[1] The Royal Shakespeare Company's production of *Restoration* transferred from the Swan Theatre, Stratford-upon-Avon to The Pit, Barbican Centre, London. Bond re-rehearsed sections of the play prior to its London opening on 29 March, 1989.

understanding and strength. I think that because of the way work is organised and homes have become more faced to the external instead of the internal, then cultural work becomes more important. Consider the USA truck drivers development of cab radio services. Technology changes artistic processes because it changes communication. Left politics is almost always late in adopting modern technologies because they are initially controlled by right-wing autocrats. *They* use them to invent fantasy; *we* can use them to create reality.

E.B.

Geoff Gillham
Canton, Cardiff   January 1991

Dear Geoff,

Thanks for sending me *The Twisting Path*.[1] I think that capitalist art
(when it isnt being sentimentally lachrymose) uses frenzy (think of pop videos) -
to cut and slash everything as if the editing were being done by a lunatic with a
razor - so that nothing has meaning or requires response, but everything has
motion and requires reaction. We need simplicity and strength, as a basis for
expansiveness and completeness. The play, though, raises difficulties for me -
which I'll try to sort out. Nothing is ever solved by an execution, by the way.
Executions are sometimes understandable but they're always a distraction from
creating a new life - and they easily become part of a reactionary mythology.
Consider the different demises of Hitler and the Romanofs. A revolution gains
nothing by vindictiveness. I think making the last emperor of China a librarian
was a sign of revolutionary strength. In a moral sense a revolution can have no
enemies except itself - and though there are immediate practical questions which
have to be dealt with, we should understand that there's always a cost to pay for
these: if there werent, a revolution wouldnt be necessary, since ideology would
have lost its mystic *and* its financial foundation!

The image of the hawk at the end [of *The Twisting Path*] I feel suspicious
about. It implies that there is something "natural" about revolution - but
revolution is entirely cultural and not inevitable; and because it's cultural it goes
through the human psyche. It's the failure to understand this that paralysed the
communist revolution: the idea that the super party would somehow do the work
of the human psyche - and had to because the human psyche was often enchained
to ideology. But (I dont want to be simplistic about this) although you can - as a
party - open prison doors you cannot make people go out through them: prisons
have their own culture and deviations - and, again, if this werent so, revolution
wouldnt be necessary. When Christianity stopped being a basis for social
stability (which within limits it had been) the industrial and financial revolutions
had created a working class that was not incorporated sufficiently in state
ideology - and so a new state ideology became necessary. A part of this was

---

[1] Bond regularly receives plays from new and established writers.

precisely to stress that people were *not* incorporatable - although God had died to make everyone human (sinless) yet everyone was - it was stressed even more strongly - imprisoned in sin: hence Calvin and predestination. It's an extraordinary paradox! And so there is a class of people outside society who are also its very foundations - the decultured working class. What to do with that class was a pressing cultural (interpretive) question - by defining the class the ruling class partly defined itself. So a super-earth presence was required - the super-heavenly presence was not enough, because that had to be paradoxical. Nietzsche invented the superman - exploited and misappropriated them: the Machiavellian blond beast was the superman. This is of course not practical! - and Nietzsche had no political programme. Hitler revolved the idea into making a "mass" become "the folk" and so a source not of worthlessness and instead a source of ultimate value! - (the contortions of ideology are always extraordinary and blatant once they're understood). He then has to provide a new menacing class - the Jews, Reds, gypsies, etc. Nietzsche was not an antisemite and abhorred the idea. The superman lead to fascism and to its own destruction. Lenin was faced though with the same problem - it was the problem of the nineteenth century: how to incorporate into the state the new body of people outside the state culture - when they were incorporated, Marx said, the state would disappear because people and state would have become one. How do you achieve this process - since it is not natural? It is not natural solely because of ideology. When we have language - then ideology becomes not only possible but inevitable - since language is more extensive than knowledge. So how? Lenin invented the superparty. Whatever his reasons for this is now not the pressing question. The superparty has failed just as the superman failed. That is a fact of practical politics. It's because ideology - which is the faith of the individual psyche - comes between action and reality. One could almost say it's the job of the psyche to frustrate theory. But many things intervene. The extraordinary productivity of modern technology swamps mind and reality with goods (to put it in that clearly impermissible way - impermissible because technology is reality).

We have to understand how it is that the "individuals" of the "mass" have to find autonomy - and the implications for art of this are enormous. Really, political theatre has discounted subjectivity because it regarded it as a bourgeois invention. But where did the bourgeoisie invent it from - is it God? Did it find subjectivity while it was having a stroll on the water? Subjectivity was heightened and intensified in the Renaissance because new social forms required it: technology made different people necessary. The invention of bourgeois subjectivity was as inevitable as the invention of the city proletariate. Both stem from the new machines. And living, working with, and consuming the product of, the new technology means that the working class develops its own subjectivity. Subjectivity isnt a fixed quality but changes historically. Subjectivity is the basis for self autonomy in the modern world. And so socialist political theatre has to accept responsibility for relating to that subjectivity - or it becomes a mere formality. A super art! And then subjectivity will create its own dialectic with that super art - and will certainly not be propagandised by it. Because political revolution is radically revolutionary in the psyche. Really it's saying to people, you have a right to *be* - and that is very revolutionary. No one said it before Marx. (Christianity certainly didnt otherwise it wouldnt have needed the Devil.)

But subjectivity isnt, I repeat, a fixed quality or quantity. Consider the subjectivity of the middle class in classical Athens. There a theory of tragedy could operate as a theory of catharsis. The hero suffered and he was your surrogate. Christianity said the same thing: Christ suffered on your behalf. But Christianity was not cathartic but redemptive. It didnt clear - but colonised. You were exonerated from sin *and* deeply captured by sin. The Athenian audience went home freed from their trauma. For their subjectivity catharsis really worked. Why? Because they were a privileged class. Just as slaves did the heavy work for them - actors could do their deep suffering. And when they went back into the city - the slaves were there (by working at the economic problems) to buttress the cathartic experience. Catharsis wasnt purely a product of art - something inherent in art - but depended on the support of slavery: not merely in the way an easel supports a painted work of art - but more profoundly: slavery was the hidden presence on the Greek stage: and the slaves were subordinated by - again a "super" - supercitizenry. This means that if you play the same play in a modern city it does not work in the same way as it did in Athens. Not merely because language has changed - but because catharsis is no longer supported by the theory that certain people are in fact two-footed cattle. And so the audience leaves the modern Greek performance - but once they're on the tube, the economic social problems return - the state of the city, of industry, the level of wages, the degree of urban violence, etc., etc., etc., etc. These practical problems ignite the imaginative problems of the psyche. And so certain problems of subjectivity are left unattended in society - and because subjectivity is never dormant but always needs a world view, subjectivity starts creating its own dialectical relationships which - if they're not generalised - may easily become reactionary or, even worse, holy. And so we cant have a political theatre - one that will really deal with the areas the "super leagues" have failed to deal with - unless it includes an expression of tragedy. Not because for a modern audience tragedy will be - could possibly be - cathartic - but because subjectivity without "rational" language becomes reactionary and destructive. Tragedy makes experience understandable and usable - and shows that what is beyond our control need not destroy us. I mentioned tragedy, but we need to look again at the whole dramatic experience. We need a form of acting and writing which presents the positions of subjectivity on stage but makes them usable and changeable and examinable - that's what I call a theory of TEs. That we can get into the climaxes - as well as the trivia - of common experience - to show how they are not determined by fate. The relations between language and emotion change just as events are given new meanings. The old dichotomy between reason and emotion is seen to be false (something which I suspect Dorothy Heathcote doesnt understand) - its dangerous form occurs in much of Bloomsburyism - and Lawrence's fascism.

I've gone into all this because I want to disagree with you about Havel. I think he's reactionary. Of course I dont deny the man's personal courage. But I read his prison letters with increasing despair. He says he cannot believe in God but has to believe in "being" - and the philosopher he relies on most is Heidegger. Now Heidegger was a Nazi. That wasnt an unfortunate error of his, an avoidable consequence of this philosophy. His notion of "being" is reactionary, and essentially so: because it posits conservative forces outside history and sees technology - not as a possible means of human liberation but as an intrusion in the sacred life of "das volk." It's the conservatives' hankering for the past: and Havel has it - deeply so. And that distorts his judgement. When he became president he walked up the aisle of some cathedral - surrounded by clerics in expensive fancy dress, and bowed to a book on the altar. No book should be bowed to - it would be better to burn books than bow to them. Perhaps Havel was bowing to the emptiness on the altar - which would be even worse? He makes an argument about language having to mean "reality." Then that trot up the aisle was an obscenity - a bowing to forces of manipulation and distortion and in the end corruption: nothing to do with respecting the truth of language. When he came to London he criticised the former Czech government for selling explosives to the Middle East - and then ceremonially reviewed Margaret Thatcher's greycoats in front of some palace - and all of those were trained to use nuclear weapons. What is the honesty-to-language in that? And now Pinter has jumped on the bandwagon. In a TV programme he said that the USAs conduct in South America was appalling - which is well said - but went on to say it's because we distort language. It isnt. It's because our governments are capitalist. And Havel is capitalising his own country. You will see that he will become increasingly reactionary. That is the logic of his position - and the drift of his nostalgia. What he venerates as "being" is precisely that complex of subjectivity which we have to open up in TEs - to make human, take from the ancient hands of gods and devils and fate and make our responsibility. And I think that is really what art does. Of course often its captured by state authority - but only because, within historical periods, those states were progressive - and so they possessed the rational in art. Tragic catharsis was once rational - and this is inscribed in Greek art, in its states and plays. Human tragedy, rational tragedy, just as human and rational laughter, would be different.

I think to support all this there has to be some understanding of the way the human mind is formed. I think children are involved in large political relationships - the securing of security among powers which are themselves autonomous. As the child has no practical understanding of the world it teaches itself saga. It interprets its experience in terms of saga - that's why traditional fairy stories were often ferocious. The imagination functions like magic - not arbitrarily (much modern literature for children tries to turn the child's saga into whimsy or fancy: it's a way of controlling children by blunting their power to question and respond). The child has to create imaginary interpretations of and solutions to its world because it cant be rational about it. Hence the child's anger and innocence: and because it's so vulnerable it creates a utopia to live in - an imaginary one - but one for which it pays the appropriate personal, cultural, subjective cost. The saga world is complete and is both lucid and tragic: and the child accepts experiences far beyond its seemingly appropriate age - not merely, as Freud found, in sex, but in culture, in all the forces of mind except maturity. As the child grows it enters a different world. This is the world of the story. The story concerns adult relationships with the autonomous world. A child's food comes to the table like manna from heaven. The adult's comes through his salary. This salary is part of an economic and technological structure. This structure has its own autonomy - its own necessity. Technology and economy depend on laws of functioning. If you have cars you have an oil industry, so you have to have tankers and pipe lines and so you need more cars and more roads to pay for the petrol and... This world of story is not a world of imagination but of fact. Of course facts are important to the child. Fire is hot for children. But they are not concerned with making sure petrol does not explode into fire. The story world requires organisation and understanding of the facts - and the more they're understood, the more organisation. And so the child grows into the world of the story and is "told the story" (in instalments) - but the child's mind is structured by experience and practice on interpreting events and people in terms of saga. One language has to learn another. If we were not vulnerable children for so much of our lives (and in the past the proportion was usually relatively much greater) we would not understand a work of art. A picture? - we would say: can you eat it? No - then burn it to turn some machine. Or to warm your hands - but to warm your mind, what does that mean...? And tragically to invite confrontation with fire!... clearly anyone who can read a work of art must be mad; it must come in the language of madness, of breakdown or so it would all be if our minds were not first established in saga. So the saga-child must learn the story of the factual world. The saga uses imagination. The story depends wholly on facts. But then something strange happens. Because the story is *owned* - politics are owned, society is owned, the machines are owned. And clearly not everyone can go everywhere to find out everything (and for long periods no one could travel into sub-atomic matter and so forth). The saga-child asked questions and made his own version of the answers (a child has to do that because it looks at the world from the outside: the child is so vulnerable that he's deeply inside and this is what it makes it see from the outside - ask anyone in prison or the first day they wear a uniform). And now for the child facts seem to be more and more autonomous and dangerous as the story is told - and imagination has less and less control over them. And so the maturing mind, or the growing mind is even more vulnerable - and it has to accept more and more on face value what even of the story it is told. Clearly if you are responsible for the story (if you and your institutions own it) you will tell the story in ways that will fit the growing child into your version of the story. And that is the strange thing - because the story is always told in terms of the saga. And it's that which is the substance of all ideology - all mystification of experience. It isnt done cynically - the pope believes in God as much as he believes in Poland as motherland and fatherland. The consequences of this are truly profound: it means that the story is told in terms of the imaginary - but the story is, as I explained, determined, it comes laden with the laws of technology and economics, and so the imagination is turned into iron facts - it becomes ineluctable. That's why Germans died for Hitler and Brits for Thatcher. Of course it's reinforced by fear and rewards but basically it's the story being told in terms of the saga. That becomes the structure of the psyche and it then describes the world in those terms and naturally believes the description it applies to it. I think what gives art its peculiar impact is that it's the effort to tell the saga in terms of the story - to reverse the usual flow of ideology. That's why art is often co-opted by ideology because it is such a powerful weapon - it goes to the seat of consciousness and psyche. I dont mean by this that I wish to see a return to the wishful imagination of the child. That's only part of the child's imagination anyway, because I think its imagination is also profound. We have to learn the story - we dont have slaves to do any of it for us. And our machines always insist we live in reality, in the story, eventually: our machines are against ideology in the end because (if I may be paradoxical) machines are interested in the true imagination and not its distortion, they're more interested in machine users than in machine owners (when the two are different). And if we dont live in reality our machines turn into bombs and other weapons. The process of culture is finding ways of understanding the story and using it and retelling it in terms of the necessity for balance and judgement of the saga. But I repeat - it's the telling of the story in terms of the saga - ideology - which really keeps people in the state of the child.

That broadly is what I see to be the function of theatre and other art. It's why I disagree with Dorothy Heathcote because I dont think it's true that the way you're taught is more important than what you're taught. And I think her use of business managers' human-relations charts is suspect. These charts depend on incorporating people into existing systems of understanding - reified versions of the story - and do not allow people to question function. So I think what she is doing is really ghettoising imagination - in a Bloomsburyite way - and not feeing it to question the ideology of the story. It does not help in teaching the child the nature of the world. The saga is confrontational. And as the story is told and learned the tragic and lucid honesty of the saga has to be retained or the child's mind becomes instrumental. The Nazis were very fond of art.

Does this make any sense? There would be other ways of describing these processes of course. I've chosen a way which clearly I've derived from my work in theatre. If it makes sense, then I think you might apply some of it to *TTP*.

Because it seems very much to do what Havel does: namely to celebrate freedom, escape from the corruption of tyranny, etc. Why does he choose "Workers of the World Unite" as the slogan for his examination of the misuse of language? The slogan is profoundly true - as profound as learning the earth's round not flat. The problem has been how to make workers unite. Lenin you remember thought they would not fight each other and for the imperialist powers in 1914. The slogan, perhaps, is not "believed" because the problem of creating understanding and unity isnt understood - the relation between story and saga, between individual, community, and ownership isnt understood (if you dont own your society you dont own the blood in your veins: as patriots make very clear). Havel doesnt deal with this. He merely says the shopkeeper who displays the slogan doesnt believe it: he seems to imply it is unbelievable - and impossible. Freedom is what you get when you throw off a dictatorship and enter the bourgeois market. Certainly Havel beyond genuflecting to Heidegger and altars has not done anything else: which is why every reactionary has jumped onto his bandwagon (I heard a radio priest describe him as the European king of philosophers). As much as I liked your play I felt it could leave an audience with some of Havel's false notions. That really is my criticism of it. I felt I was free to admire the play - though I'd rather they'd looked at the stones than the hawk at the end: what does the hawk know of carrying stones, but those who carry stones can learn they are beautiful - just as the condemned may notice the post on which they are tied is made of beautiful wood - but my freedom derived from a saga-version of the story: and will your audience have that?

I hope these remarks are of some use. I repeat: I liked the play very much. Im asking you to do more, that's all...

Best wishes,

Edward Bond

Hilde Klein

Malaga, Spain   8 August 1991

Dear Hilde,

    Thanks for your letter.

    Dr. Hema Raghavan seems to be a very kind and warm-hearted person. She is right in saying that the real victims of Western wars are the Eastern and Middle Eastern poor - and the culturally poor in the West. I've contributed an article on a book called "Authors on the Gulf War" - which is supposed to be published shortly. I dont know if they'll print my article. When I return home I will send you a copy. The series of twentieth century big wars was inaugurated by the promise of a "war to end wars." Since then wars have become bloodier and even - usually - more pointless. We now have designer wars. You massacre many enemies and even sacrifice a few of your own soldiers. Consumerism is thus given a moral purpose - and this makes it easier to ignore the peace-time exploitation and abuse of the non-Western poor.

    About Dr. Raghavan's remarks on violence. Im a little nonplussed. She suggests that perhaps we should not deal with what she acknowledges is the pressing problem: violence. What is our reason for if not to combat unreason? Like her I am worried by the violence that saturates Western entertainment medias. But very little of it is cathartic. It is ideological - it enforces illusions about innate violence and sanctions law-and-order as a substitute for morality. Far from being cathartic, it promotes social fears and hatreds. The Greeks saw violence visited on them by their Gods and the almost abstract nature of the world. The modern media select specific targets - the psychotically ill and the socially deprived. Both are seen as beyond the reach of human change. The fears they rouse cannot be quieted by catharsis.

    My own use of violence is not meant to be cathartic (as it's usually understood) - violence is always part of the problem and not of the solution, even when it is revolutionary. I show violence as oppression, as implicit in society not nature - but as society is a cultural product, it is changeable. I think that over the centuries the nature and justifications of violence have changed (Hitlerism was in this sense a reversal because it took its ideology seriously: it had "natural enemies," confused culture with nature). I think we can use violence rationally in the theatre - we show its reality but destroy its rationalizations and glamorizations. We cant do that well enough yet: if we could we could solve the problem. What we mustnt do is ignore - or trivialize - the problem because then we "solve" it by ignoring it. Art has to be desperate or it has very little to say. That means reproducing the problem in order to make the handling of it desperate. What is cathartic is not emotional release but the rational description and analysis of violence. Obviously this isnt unemotional, abstractly logical reason - the reason that comes from involvement in the crisis - it is when reason is made to be involved in the crisis - to acknowledge it from the inside - that reason becomes cathartic - because it is not a mere emptying but a creation: reason begins to work against madness and violence - and the imperative comes from, or at least is empowered by, the ability to describe from within. But the pity is that we are still so confused about these things - still abstractly see reason and emotion as opposed. Reason never works on its own, it is always the expression of values - and the values are changeable. The problem about that is that human beings and their society are a continuum - the individual is the expression of the whole and does not exist outside it. Change is possible - indeed, inevitable - because the whole, society, is itself in tension: and it creates the autonomous individual as part of that tension.

Dr. Raghavan also wonders whom we address. Wisdom always exists in a diaspora - but that means that it can be found anywhere. And most people are usually wiser than they are allowed to be or dare to be - they think their wisdom is a weakness. They have no one to talk to them about it - or help them to put it into a wider sphere. They know that their society abuses rational processes - making them mechanical and reinforcing them with consumer values. Most destructive people are only so by a sort of opportunism - they are part of a violent culture or sub-culture. They are not violent by belief or principle; that is almost always left to people in authority. What is surprising is that by now they have not yet blown the world to bits. The only reason they havent is the - in spite of everything - wisdom of ordinary people in the streets, with all its imperfections and illusions. Human beings will always seek understanding, always question - that is innate in the acts of cognition themselves. That intellectuality is prior to emotion but may be corrupted, distorted by it.

About the Beckett story. A Beckett story always suggests an Anti-Beckett story which is better - it is almost a law of literature and human decency. It is true that if two people lie together they warm one another and if they lie alone they freeze. Of course, animals know this. Unfriendly dogs - who scrap by day -

will sleep together when the dark comes. Horses stand side by side to shut out the wind. The herd gathers when the weather turns for the worst. But suppose two people are shot and thrown into the mass grave - still half alive - in the massacre and they cling to one another as they die? The soldiers who machine gun them may also put their arms round each other, for spiritual comfort. What do we gather from this? The same act may promote violence or humane caressing. You have to understand the situation. Otherwise we just do what dogs do. This is my argument against Beckett - that the situation is forgotten.

Best wishes,

Edward Bond

Benjamin May
Horsham, West Sussex   16 September 1991

Dear Benjamin May,

I understand your concern with nuclear weapons. They are still the greatest threat to human life. The collapse of eastern communism doesnt alter that. That collapse could even add to the tensions in the world: it depends how reactionary the new governments will be. It's not that they will arm themselves with their own nuclear weapons - though even that is possible - but that they will add to the amount of reaction and nihilism in the world - and so add to its bigotry and desperation. As Asia becomes more industrialised, capitalism will run out of cheap submissive labour. In the West, socialism isnt "necessary" while capitalism can provide enough goods to mollify discontent. The *economic* thrust for change is lacking. In Asia there will be a new problem. The problem of Eastern European communism was that it was grafted (by Lenin) onto a feudal consciousness and culture: the stage of non-conformist religion, of bourgeois organisation and administration, was missing. In Asia the lack is even more significant. It might be that the political changes which will be caused by industrialisation will align with strange chillastic forms of religion and nationalism.

The oddity of capitalism is that it strives for perfection of technology but has a human philosophy which is based on our imperfection, our radical animality. It is a strange combination - and it is used to justify inequality and injustice. Human beings have usually had a vision of an ideal state, a utopia, a heavenly garden - Marx, even, had the notion of a past golden age (surely a mistake, which simplifies the real problem of rebuilding the future). This vision is being replaced with the notion of law and order, of improving discipline - not of eradicating evil. *That* is as innate (it is held) as work-shyness. And so we are institutionalizing the dangerousness and destructiveness of human beings. We try to found justice on a philosophy of injustice. It is a form of social Darwinism. I dont think a continuing society can be built on such a paradox. The nearer to perfection technology comes, the more imperfect and anti-social human beings will be seen to be. Those who are socially adept will, in simple fact, depend on exploiting the "inferiority" of other people - the unsuccessful, the lazy, the socially derelict. It is surprising how the rhetoric is used by the conservative

minded: they talk so easily and angrily of hoodlums, misfits, criminal elements...
One wonders: if the parents are always to blame, what is the justification of
punishing anybody? If the parents are to blame: that means that the home
authority is to blame? Then why arent the city authority, the national authority
also to blame? - why should all authority outside the home be blameless? If it is a
question of authority and not genuine discontent with authority, who lays down
the dividing line at the door to the house? The real problem is that national
authority has espoused a destructive philosophy. It submits human will to the
mechanisms of the market. If it wants to ameliorate some of the worse effects of
the market (is *that* the difference between Thatcher and Major?) it does this in
conflict with its own philosophy: it will not deal with the cause but only the
effect.

   The philosophy authorises one form of rapacity and violence and
condemns another. The mechanical institutions of the market - and the culture,
the "life styles" they support - are rapacious and destructive. When people
outside this culture - and without cultural access to the institutions - react, by way
of riot and crime, they are condemned. This contradiction must be destructive. It
seems that instead of revolutions being caused only - mainly? - by economic need
and change, they will be caused by cultural need, human deprivation - by having
to live with the spectacle of rampant injustice, of diverging class cultures. The
discontent this creates is met by an already articulated argument, the one on
which the institutions that caused the discontent are based: some people are
inferior, some people matter, some dont. All human psyche is fuelled by the
early contrasts between the child and the adult, the powerless and the powerful.
This creates a speculative, chancy attitude to life - on which the firmest
foundations of human culture are based. The curious to-ing and fro-ing of Gods
and humans in Homer: the will of the gods is fate - but it always accords with the
"character," the will, of the individuals, the humans. Conservativism is like that:
it takes human characteristics and infers an inevitability from them. But you
could equally well argue that the characteristics of the Homeric gods are inferred
from the humans. And yet it's in defiance of the Gods that the Greeks -
eventually - learned to create their humanity: they made something firm out of the
chance encounters, out of the arbitrary they made human law. This isnt mere
defiance, because it is based on the human need to state a law of humanity in the
face of the apparent chaos of the universe and the inhuman discipline of the (now)
market institutions. How often fairy stories begin with a trip to market - that is

the factual, mechanical basis of life - and then the supernatural, the sexual, the human need intervenes and turns the market transaction into a human theatre. It is in *that* theatre that the need for revolution is made apparent - not merely in the economic world of the market. Yet the two are absolutely connected - and any division made between them leads to an ideology which imposes itself on the powerless or to anarchic aestheticism.

The position of the theatre, now, is this: the economic isnt seen, socially, as a source of change - it provides goods that stupefy the need for change. So, it is argued, the economic, the social, no longer connects with the theatre as it did before. The human spirit can be examined in and for itself. The story does not begin with the journey to market. This is the "new" theatre - but of course it's merely the return of the more banal part of the theatre of the sixties. It isnt new, this sudden interest in non-communication, in the merely aesthetically satisfying or provocative, in the world of desire that relates only to its own fetishes and images. Not even children do that!

So we still have to take the road to market - and meet the genie, the stranger, the disaster on the way. That is the basic shell of human life and it cant be changed: but the contents always change - and it's by understanding and using the contents of the situation that we make art. It is also the situation of human life in general: human beings are not a stomach that eats, they are a psyche that eats. To refer to Homer again, it's what you find in the last book of the *Iliad*. Achilles and Priam meet and exchange their symptoms of humanity, their deference to the Gods, their human need - and then eat. Our theatre must be of this world, the (at the moment) market mechanisms - nor must we escape into an abstract world of spirit and effect.

The way to approach this in theatre is to see that human beings (and so roles) are made of two elements: the idiosyncratic and the ideological. Political theatre tends to concentrate on the ideological because it wants to free people from ideological blindness. I suppose all readings of the world are in some sense blind: the mythical ideologies of past worlds have always been rooted in the best science and technology of the day, they always had to be if they were to be effective (except at those moments when society collapsed into its worst nightmares - but these were always times of collapse, not building). So there is no "pure sighted" ideology to counterpose to the false ruling ideology. That isnt so much of a problem: we dont have to understand all, we have to understand more. But the idiosyncratic isnt distinct from the ideological, it is partly formed by it: our minds are part of the world, not merely part of our body. Yet they are also our reaction to the world: we become part of it by that reaction - we learn to do that from what we're reacting against, inevitably (we dont have private worlds). So we mustnt discount the idiosyncratic as irrelevant or subordinated to the ideological: it is part of it but also potentially critical of it as well as merely reproducing it in its own idiosyncratic terms. The idiosyncratic is close to what I call radical innocence (which seeks the firmness in mere chance that I spoke of above, and tries to assert law against the chaotic and arbitrary).

At the moment the ideological seems to be reaffirmed (because communism collapses in the East). So (it is said) the idiosyncratic may be indulged - that is the new theatre. But then it merely mystifies - it doesnt accept or record or deal with the pain of the idiosyncratic, its struggle, its danger, its cursing of others, its infiltration by ideology. You can only deal with the idiosyncratic properly in a social theatre - not an aesthetic or merely hedonistic theatre of "desire." As if human beings knew what they desired! - or that desire was the ultimate for them in that it could ever be fulfilled! I see a new theatre as being freed from a false ideological struggle with a false ideology. But the triumphing ideology - capitalism - remains false: it hasnt proved its superiority in any way, because it remains bound to its own destructiveness - it is still the harbinger of nightmares. But we should now be able to see very clearly that political theatre cannot be reduced to the merely economic or ideological: it must deal with the idiosyncratic as well, as the bridge between the inhuman and the human. Ideology is concealed in it and has to be hunted out where it is: but it is also the source of the need to hunt it out - it is the criticism of ideology, the radical imperative. This comes not from the gut but from the psyche. And there is nothing spiritual about this: there is much more danger of even progressive ideology being merely spiritual, in spite of all its talk of the socially concrete.

Of course, human beings are concerned with their desires. But they are not the main definer of being human. Human beings proceed from their radical need to question (which creates their primary world of the stories) and this always extends to the boundary - first to the room, then the home, and then the world beyond. The idiosyncratic is in fact the expression of that need to understand the totality of things and explain it in philosophy and story, and act out the relation to it in intellect and drama. (Before Descartes describes his searches into basic knowledge he stage-sets: the room he is in, the chair, his emotional and psychic state - and his own emotional reactions to what he learns: it is Hamlet to the life.)

So there is an outward thrust from the infant to the aged, from the idiosyncratic to the ideological, from the personal to the public - this is an absolute constituent of the human psyche. But it can at any stage, from infant autism to elder statesman paranoia be halted and turned back on itself; and then it starts to create reality in its own image, the ideological becomes a map, then, on which the real is manipulated. Oscar Wilde had some of this idea when he said that life imitated art - but he saw it mainly in the sequence ideology-idiosyncratic, whereas in the case of real people it is often in the sequence idiosyncratic-ideological (the individual turns back from reality in fear). The trajectory from idiosyncratic to ideology isnt what theatre portrays (or copies from life) but it is itself the very process of theatre: theatre can certainly use the idiosyncratic but should not itself be idiosyncratic - it should always be (truly) ideological. The so called "new" theatre is purest idiosyncracy.

I hope these remarks make some sense to you. Really they are the fruit of what I've been thinking about while I lived on the boat. I now want to embody it in new plays. I hope you're well - and that your questioning has become a source of strength now, and not of doubt or frustration. Im sorry that all I can do is share some of my ideas with you. I would like to do more, but I don't have a theatre to do it in!

Yours sincerely,

Edward Bond

Hilde Klein

Malaga, Spain   9 March 1992

Dear Hilde,

I didnt much like the NT *Sea*.[1] The young director has a reputation for ability; really he has energy, a collection of tricks and self-assurance. He is exploited by those who run our theatres. He knows little about acting. He is good on spectacle. In our economy the packaging is more important than the content. It is a matter of time before we eat the biscuit box rather than the biscuits - the box will be more attractive and probably more nutritional. I went to a few rehearsals otherwise the production would have been worse. Interestingly, the director understands more about things (scenery, props, lights) than people (the actors and their characters). That is what makes him persona grate in a theatre dedicated to not understanding theatre. He does have real talent, but he is not yet in touch with it and may lose it.

I've read the comments by Hema Raghavan that you kindly sent me. Really I think she is making my point. I see no glamour in political violence - and nor is violence a rite of passage to maturity for colonised or oppressed people. And little can be done - creatively - by political violence. It is at best a means of immediate defence against intolerable oppression. But this means that sometimes the organisation of political violence is justified: this is so in certain South American countries under vicious right-wing tyrannies. But it is never more than a crutch for a lame man. Nor should its victories be celebrated: they cost too much for rejoicing. We can leave that to Stalin and Thatcher. Satyagraha depends on its ability to change others by example or by provoking guilt in them; more active non-violence depends on the objective limits of the power that is being opposed - that there just arent enough police (for example) to deal with the crisis. There are those who will not be changed by a passive example: your nonviolent "weakness" will be taken as an example of your inferiority and in fact justify the violence used against you. The doctrinaire - like the righteous - do not feel guilt. And weapons are now so sophisticated and

---

[1] *The Sea*, directed by Sam Mendes, opened in the Lyttleton, Royal National Theatre on 12 December, 1991. My examination of this production appears in "Edward Bond and Britain's National Theatre." *Contemporary British Theatre* ed. Theodore Shank, London: Macmillan, 1993.

ruthless that there is little objective limitation to government power. Since the second world war the great military states have been defeated only by guerrillas. Given this situation do you have a right to defend not yourself but those for whose well-being you are morally responsible? Ghandi said let the Nazis gas your children: it is there that I draw the line. Satyagrahis would argue that in the long run (because of the reasons above) fewer children will suffer and the world will be more just. I dont think so - tyranny is paranoid and there is no limit to its appetite for victims. This is the only justification for the use of political violence.

But even this leaves many questions unanswered. The running of liberal democracy in fact involves considerable violence - though physical violence only as a last resort. But it is physical violence that is provoked by the culture and the system: consider the massacre that ended the intervention in Iraq (which is very seldom acknowledged in the West). Democracy seems to want revenge against its enemies just as it wants scapegoats amongst its own citizens. The relationship between psychology and political structures is not understood - because governments still make themselves responsible for communal morality - and this means that morality is then always used to justify their overlordship. We run our existence badly. What ought to happen in the psyche we try to act out in political structures: and what ought to belong to political structures we try to incorporate in the human psyche. But as these things change their places - being in the wrong place - they change their quality: they become corrupt. It is not that there is an evil action which can be performed either by an individual or by the state: the one act changes its nature when it is performed by the wrong agency. I'll try to explain this a little more. But it's worth looking at the symptoms of this at the present time.

Thirty years ago public morality had to do with personal guilt. This was connected with personal sin. To be an unmarried mother was a sin. To shoplift was a sin (not just a crime). To be a street hooligan was a sin. Theft was a sin. So was drunkenness. And so on. Now there has been a change. Unmarried motherhood, homosexuality, greed - these are no longer (officially) regarded as sins. Society permits them. That is a very radical change: and it's reflected to a considerable extent in the public media. Young people now have a new concern. It's now ecological damage, the failure of the economy, the creation of new diseases. These are not sinful things issuing from the self - they are social phenomena. And curiously, they are the phenomena of wartime. It's in war that we say: the land is laid waste, inner cities are destroyed (by bombs), there are the new diseases of starvation and arbitrary congregation. I think that, for young people, the apprehensions are not of personal sin or guilt - they are to do with social phenomena. We live in peace but have the fears, dreads and apprehensions appropriate to war - of course the threats are a little way off, not so immediate as a bomber flying overhead, but in some way even more threatening. The bomber can be identified - shot down (by counter violence). But the destruction to the earth and sky and sea - the creation of the signs of war - is inherent in the way we enjoy peace, in our economic system. Economic recession is a "war symptom" because it creates a lack of social goods (though again, at a slight remove: it doesnt entail rationing, except by purse). So we are asked to be more economically active... but this can only produce more of the social and ecological signs of war. In the past to be good - without sin - meant observing certain personal forms of conduct. Now to be good we have to be (in the wider, long-term - but increasingly that becomes more short-term) bad. In a military war you are clearly either a friend or foe (unless, of course, you appear as a friend but are really a foe - a spy or saboteur or some other sort of traitor). But young people now have to be both friend-and-foe of the society-and-world. They are divided against themselves: and this is a requirement of living in a liberal democracy founded on capitalist economics. A sinful person may have faith - and hope to escape from sin while still acknowledging that much of what he or she does is sinful: this is the torment of the saint. But in the economic relation there is no escape: you must be good-and-bad in the one person - the economic imperative is opposed to the ecological imperative.

This creates two sorts of wounded - again, the wounded of peace resemble the wounded of war. There are the walking wounded: those who survive in the economic battle. But they are damaged: they are friend-and-foe of the society-world. Faith cannot create a balance for them, as it could for the sinner. Instead they have a fanaticism: they believe that their society is wholly right (not that they are sinners, half wrong). This is what creates the reactionary politics of liberal democracy. When the economy fails, reaction wants scapegoats - or even just random victims as targets of anger. I think that capitalist societies do not create "culture," they are living off the culture of the past, off the fading lights of the enlightenment. In themselves they are barbarising - and that is the cause of the increasing barbarity of the *law-living* citizens of the U.S.A. The economic system produces - through its mediation through the psyche - barbarism: and so the increasing reaction of American politics - the death penalty, the Reagan desocializing of the community. Spiritually the U.S.A. is parasitic on the past - and the past is dead. A corpse will not sustain life for long. And so American religion becomes more aggressive - more socially destructive. Recently a serial killer's trial was TV-ed. He was ritualistically abused by his victim's relatives. Then he made a statement. He was "okay when he had Jesus - he went wrong when he lost Jesus - now he's going to a penitentiary and he'll live Jesus again." No one pointed out that most of those who do not have Jesus do not in fact kill serially: there was no informed commentary in the court, merely barbarism and misleading ritual. But this has taken me from the walking wounded - the jury, the judge, the good citizens watching it on TV, those who survive society - to the severely wounded: often their anti-socialness has been at first stimulated by a just criticism of society - but as this was unorganised and uninformed, and as society was so monolithic and so righteous, the severely wounded become the pure-foes of society. Though even they may adhere to society's mores in thought if not in act: thus prisoners often say they deserve to be punished - they support death-penalties and say they strayed from Jesus. So even when the faults seem to be personal - as personal as sin - the cause is to be found within society. Maybe a reformed society would still produce its foes - but we cant say this or know this till society is reformed - and then the actions we take against the anti-social will not be reactionary, counter-productive - we will have learned to care for our enemies and be strong enough to do so without risk. This is a society of violence - in a stalinist police-state the violence is largely physical - in a liberal democracy it is largely cultural, psychological, economic. But it produces victimism - just as stalinism produces the prisoners of work-camps. Unfortunately, liberal democracy's philosophy justifies it in blaming it's victims - and so the tyranny is disguised. But clearly if all the nations of the world were run in this way - with the same economic system - there could be no peace: the system creates and needs its enemies and even its friends are also its foes.

We can only understand violence when we understand this situation: that violence is not the expression of innate aggression. We have the capacity to aggress - but the capacity is always under-determined - it needs a social cause and a social stimulus if it is to occur. And often it can incorporate forms of protest and resistance into the system by which it itself is maintained.

I said that social structures become a process which ought to be psychological - that society is acting out relationships which really should occur in individual minds. I will try to explain. The child cannot understand its world unless it is told fictions, fables - sometimes lies. A fable - like a myth - takes a truth and wraps it in a lie: in an attempt to make it comprehensible or livable with. It tries to pin down a mystery - often an urgent mystery. To the child the question "why are we alive" is as urgent as the question - to society and the detective force - of why someone is dead. There is an intellectual-and-emotional urgent need for answers. But the world cannot be explained logically to a child (economics, history, science, etc.) even if all of its problems could be illuminated logically - many couldnt. The child's situation is very political: a vulnerable being surrounded by great powers. So the foundations of mind - of character - are created as a sort of drama: the world is interpretable by stories. So the human mind must be led by true-fictions into its dramatic being: it takes on many of the aesthetic characteristics of the world which its questions seek to explain or make explainable. Later the child's mind must become adult. In societies which have a close, natural relation to the earth - uncomplicated societies with simple economies and technologies - the child drama may be easily transferred to the adult-mind. The rite of passage will be expressed in the language of the child's drama - this will take on a greater seriousness, but will be continuous with the adult mind. The web of mythology and ritual action will join child and adult in the one history, the one set of stories, the one unbroken cultural source. In complicated societies this is not so. Society will own complex technologies and be sustained by complex economies. The child's drama cannot easily be transferred to these. The new systems will not have the natural aesthetics of the child's mind - as they would in a simpler society, where the earth sustained the old myths. In the simpler community the drama of the mind is the drama of society and its relation to the earth. There is no critical break. The child becomes fully adult by interpreting (and ritually being helped to interpret) the world in terms of its own existing knowledge and psyche-language. It doesnt need to impose this on the social system: the social system comes speaking the same language, articulating it into a more stable, sustaining social structure. This isnt possible in a complex society: the social and economic processes are not "natural" but technological and legalistic and multi-administrative. So the more complex and technological the social structure, the more it denies the truth of itself and talks to its members in the language of the child. It sees society in terms of the child's world - not of the adults. In a simpler society this problem just doesnt arise: the drama is continuous in meaning and performance. Primitive religions may, for example, use the surface story of the child's mind - the relationship to parents - and incorporate it into its religion: God the father etc. - or the beneficent spirits. The infra-structure of the child's mind - the fears and fantasies - can also be used - notably to create the gods of evil - also as part of the father. Really the Christian god is not a trinity but a tetrad. The fourth figure is the devil, but this becomes the individual, the believer with all his or her sin. (It also ignores the woman: really she is the Holy Ghost, that which has the gift of tongues - the mother tongue: the paternalism of the Old Testament couldnt allow a role for women - but inevitably Catholicism has to recreate her - the Virgin Mary - and the paternalism of Puritan-capitalism remove her - she becomes the witch.) - And now (because of the cultural vacuum and - probably - the opportunism of capitalist culture - as in the way it promotes crime) we have women priests. This has an importance for drama. My argument is: that the complex state images itself in the language and drama of the child - the motherland, the fatherland, duty, etc., and the child's notions of good and naughty. This is child-like! In tragedy no one is evil - that is what makes it so terrible and why a society without tragedy is not culturally mature but must create violence.

So a psychological structure is wrongly externalised - and makes the human mind its victim. Conversely, the objective structure - the factual running of the world - is internalised - the mind is seen as an object to be engineered (by stalinist politics) or medicated (liberal's gesture of tolerance to the less severely peace-war "wounded"). The world - objectively - does not need art: the human mind needs art. The child's mind incorporates the objective structures of the world - colours, movement - as in wind, storm, birds, flowers, (which bloom and fade) - into its own, initiating dramas: if the external world had a perceiving mind, then what we see as aesthetics (the bird's colours for example) would be to it merely scientific instruments or processes - like push-buttons or chemical processes: we cannot be human unless we misinterpret the world, turn it inside out and see it as having a meaning for us. Meaning becomes the tensions and epithenies of the child's mind - its dramas. This should not be projected onto the objective structures - when we are adults - in the way a child must. We need an art which enables the individual adult mind to elucidate, experience its structures in terms of its being, certainly, but not by trying to humanize its structures. This humanizes the child - but when adults try it, it dehumanizes them. *We* can have no rite of passage into our adult world - because drama should be continuous for us - and should be elucidated in dramatic forms - which certainly can see the world as absurd - but not obscenely absurd as in contemporary drama, where absurdity is indifferent to human suffering and denies meaning. Meaning is how we live - not what we live for. There is no external reason for living: we create it in our living.

Capitalist-economics use drama-art as a commodity to sustain the economic system, to weld the individual and society to the objective structure: thus it cannibalizes the adult mind by whittling it down, frivolizing it, into a child-like state: it makes the adult regressive - it talks of ownership and consumption with all the hectic urgency, belligerence, and haranguing of the nursery.

I am not saying that art is the province of the child-mind and therefore inferior to the economic cycles of reality. We have yet - as a species - to find the human relation of the adult mind to the child mind. The adult is not free to be his or her own child - either economically or psychologically - or politically or culturally. We do not yet know how to tackle ourselves seriously enough as part of a universal comedy. Our pain and tragedy are real - as are our pleasure and happiness. Now we are still trapped in our egos - and capitalist-economics lock us into our egos. Culture relates us to our world by exposing it to us - freeing it from our egos. But capitalism does not create culture - it reifies its economic processes and forms of ownership in terms of the infant's mind - it is parasitic and envious.

The child cannot know everything: its stories are like myths - they make the facts acceptable but still keep them in tension (myths do not explain away things for the same reason that religions do not abolish prayer or meditation. Obviously if there were a God there would be no need of prayer). The adult's understanding is new. The tension of the myth or fairy story must be released into tragedy and comedy - the adult cannot go away to weep in the corner or play in the street - the adult world has no escapes because it is all centre. This is the playing-and-living yard of art. Stalinist political engineering bans freedom from art in order to create it in the community: this is because it is fighting its enemies rather than creating its friends. Political freedom cannot be achieved unless the mind is free to publicly act its dramas - otherwise it becomes the victim of the obscene instead of relating itself to the objective. The passage from childhood to adulthood is not without its crises - and would not be even were it continuous, told in the same language. The child's story accepts tragedy and conflict into its meaning of the world: it takes its place in the child's mind - either as the conscious story or as an unacceptable infra-structure - unacceptable, of course, largely not because the child cant accept it but because the adults wont - it isnt convenient to the adult world. Greek theatre got near to being an appropriate theatre for its society: ours is largely inappropriate. For the child's mind drama is associated with meaning and it adopts the child's mental energy. Our theatre (along with other ideational arts) tries to use energy without meaning: consume it, make it a product - and this makes it a form of violence because it denies meaning when energy has become the expression of the need for meaning.

Clearly I do not see violence as a solution of the problem of becoming human. Because of the abused conflict between our two stages of mind (the child's and the adult's) our species will react in violence however much some of us practice Satyagraha. (I think a lot of violence was necessary in order to enable Ghandi to practice being peaceful. I do not say this cynically.) We have to understand the (structural) human drama: it is inherent in our minds as they are in our society. Both objective and subjective dramas are real: one must not be acted out in the sphere of the other. But both violence and Satyagraha do this. Satyagraha is, I think, a form of violence because it extends the child's drama not - as capitalism does - into the objective relations of the world (the physical nature of industry and money-systems, all of which have their own logic and consequences) but into the world of religion - and this dangerously debases human values. God does not create the world but destroys it. All religions try to imprison the adult in the child's drama - instead of letting that drama recreate the world. The only thing I can recognise as catharsis is a new idea. The only thing I recognise as drama is a new idea that works. Satyagraha and violence will not change the world for the better - they are merely temporary accommodations to the brutality of man-made facts. People will resort to both until we understand existence better and become that understanding.

I hope these remarks will be of some use to you.

Yours sincerely,

Edward Bond

Corrente Katiuscia

Toscana, Italy   3 June 1992

Dear Ms. Katiuscia,

Thank you for your letter. I will try to answer your questions.

Am I still a socialist? Yes. By socialism I mean that there are rational explanations of why we have problems and catastrophes - history can be understood rationally - and that we can rationally amend and improve our situation. The alternative is to have a negative or religious view of human life. You would have to believe that we are naturally and inevitably wicked or destructive - and that human reason and the human ability to love and befriend and care will always be destroyed by these two other things. Strangely, early in history human beings developed the idea of utopia as a way of facing their fear and saving their psyche from the ravages of anger and revenge. But the gap between utopia and the present could only be bridged by religion and not practical action. In this way the vision of utopia became the way in which people were condemned to the miseries of the present. If a utopian vision led to practical action, the results of that action (when it succeeded) were destroyed by the ground of that action: the religious or other worldly nature of utopia. An obvious example is Luther, who began as a revolutionary and ended as a reactionary. Revolutions fail not only for practical reasons - they live out the limitations within the original vision.

Utopia ought not to inspire hope but knowledge - it should be a practical programme, and revolutionary change should always be measured against the practical and not against the visionary. Otherwise the gap between the vision and reality will widen: inevitably the vision will drive people on to failure. We should base our present activities on a rational philosophy and not on the reaction of capitalism - because its utopia is pessimistic: that human nature is inevitably corrupt. So capitalist affluence is to provide goods, luxury, for corrupt people? And if human nature is corrupt, the entrepreneurs of capitalism are corrupt. So it's argued that a set of laws and punishments can abstractly control the human situation independently of human corruption, even of human will. The "system" is the invisible hand which manipulates people as if they were puppets. The failure of this philosophy is that it creates the psychology, the culture, of those it directs - and so it is the system which is corrupting, even if it were technically perfect and infinitely produced the goods of commerce. The evidence for this is most clearly seen in the USA - a society becoming increasingly barbarous - not merely in "riots" but in the vicious superficiality of its religion, the exploitative terror of its commerce, the nihilism of its culture. It prevents rational thought and invokes reaction. So now there is the possibility of political mavericks - people who come from nowhere (usually either the gutter or the bank) and recite populist slogans that are supposed to be cures for the ills of the system. These demagogues are very dangerous - necessarily fascistic because they will try to impose an impractical vision by violence: really they are the deliriums and hallucinations of a political fever. This is possible only because socialist politics are seen as impractical - and as without philosophical justification.

And so there has to be a philosophy not based on magic and violence. That would be socialist - and I do not think we have yet seen it. The only nations where socialism has been attempted were economically and politically unready for it. They sometimes became impositions of violence and conformity. I will try to explain why. Some of the reasons are very obvious: thus communism was imposed on much of eastern Europe after the second world war - there was no genuine revolutionary impetus to change. The imposition inevitably strengthens the opposition. But in other countries the reasons are more complex. Socialism is a philosophy of history: it says that we can rationally understand history - not that history itself is rational in a Hegelian way. But socialism is also a human practice. The trouble is that Soviet governments thought they were dealing with history and not with people. I could say that it is better for a revolution to fail than for it to make history prior to people: this is an attempt to force history to take a short cut and it cannot be done. History is mediated through people - and this is the terrain of distortion.

The only alternative to socialism is barbarism - all other political philosophies must create barbarism because they are irrational. I could say much more about this but instead I must refer you to the commentary on *The War Plays* and its account of the relationship between us and machines.[1] Machines now operate on us and our societies and psyches as the forces of natural selection - and in this sense we are made by our machines and the economic and social system

---

[1] *The War Plays*, London: Methuen, 1991.

which owns the machines. The systems that we have at the moment are irrational and so the use of machines tends towards barbarism; of course some machines are good (hospital machines) and others usually bad (weapons) - but this isnt my point: Im talking about the totality of machines and the way they are owned - it is this which enables the machines to impose barbarism on us, cultural degeneration of the sort seen in the USA. But these are points I make throughout all my work.

The problem then becomes: what are the practical means for achieving socialism? At the moment there seem few. The Soviet system has failed (as I said it was doing in my play *Lear*) - the ex-Soviet states seem bent on Thatcherism. Havel told John Major that his (Major's) recent election win was a "Victory for common sense." The win was an oddity - it meant that education, health, social institutions, cultural opportunities, were being returned to a state of fifty years ago - and worse, because there was not even any left-wing utopian opposition vision. Yet the voters could not stop themselves doing this - partly because they were misinformed but also because of a loss of conviction, a failure of will and imagination, and because of fear. It was a victory not celebrated even by the victors. But I think this is an intermediate state. A new sort of organisation has to be found - created within society. This will be a gradual process - but it will be inevitable, even if it is accompanied by an increasing reaction and barbarisation. I think the ecological consequences of affluence will be very influential - combined with the inevitable innovations of new generations. This is because the child's mind always leads to states of contradiction and contrast, as it develops into the adult mind. In our species, each new generation must be the intellectual enemy of the older generation - that is built into the nature of mind and psyche - it is really the only inevitable fact about human beings, the only thing that can be called necessary "human nature": all the other apparently natural things are merely contingent and secondary - though they *are*, as a generalisation practically inevitable (very often); yet the setting in which they operate (Im talking about the basic "instincts") changes and it is this that is culturally defining, not the instincts themselves.

A changing world will require us to organise ourselves in new ways - and the natural scepticism of youth (really this scepticism comes from the imposition of fairy stories on the facts of history - not what one might have assumed the origin of scepticism to be!) will result in new social organisations. The method isnt something that I can define now - though I could speculate, but havent the time to.

The role of my plays in this situation? I've begun to clarify this in *Olly's Prison* - filmed (not very satisfactorily) by BBC-TV to be shown later this year.[2] I've made a stage version which will be published at about the same time.[3] I dont regard the plays as utopian (though in a way they are) because this will be misunderstood. I regard utopia as practical - that is, without the combination of violence-and-magic. If the human psyche is forming itself in new ways, then my plays can co-operate with this formation. They can allow people to think and see differently. The audience doesnt necessarily have to accept the play as a whole. Perhaps smaller parts and sections will have an influence on them - either positive or negative. That's part of making utopia rational and practical. But I would add something else - which I believe I touched on in my last letter to you. A play is an "event" in its own right, and not merely as being about something itself in real life. The play itself is a real event in real life and involves the spectator as totality - not merely invoking, say, a judgement of the plays - "I liked it or didnt like it, was amused, made angry, etc." It is these states which are important - the real effects of theatre - and not what the spectator thinks about these states. I regard this fact as being of great importance. The spectator is involved in this way often in spite of him or her self: the spectator is involved in an action - and this inevitably involves him in the movement of the social-psyche - the collective movement of conflict and amity, which is the historical movement. I think this is really why societies have theatres, dramas - and is the reason for many other sorts of art: as it seems to create the most personal response it is - in fact - making the spectator a "member of history," objectify his or her position (this is why I think the rationalizing of Brecht is a mistake - the rational theatre is more penetrating. I should immediately add that Brecht's plays have an effect different from that which he theorized for them - his theory was largely negative, based on opposition to the existing theatre). I think Postmodernism makes it clear that the aesthetic is a fundamental part of human reasoning, not something consequent upon reasoning: when this is understood, the aesthetics become, of course, much more than aesthetics - we could not have the word "god" if we could not draw him. Utopia is the present - it is just that the future has to be more practical about

---

[2] *Olly's Prison* was filmed by the BBC in December 1991 but not transmitted until May 1993.

[3] *Olly's Prison*, London: Methuen, 1993.

it. That is why my history plays are about people and my epic plays about the kitchen and the street.

Yours sincerely,

Edward Bond

Phil Church

Redditch, Worcestershire   10 February 1993

Dear Phil Church,

Thanks for finding time in your Christmas break from school to reply to me so promptly. It seemed to me that "awe" and "wonder" are in themselves passive. I remember in the cold war how spirit manufacturers advised Vodka by saying the reds drank it... W and A seemed to promote attitudes, they have a religiosity which I find a ground of ignorance. Awe at a nuclear power station and the sun going down behind it. Wonder at the way gothic architects refined the arch - and at the economic system which now places a shop in every church, hospital... school, prison, morgue, graveyard... in time. So really I want to begin with curiosity. Yet this can be as destructive as awe and wonder - because it can be merely taking the clock to bits. Of course authority is adept at using wonder and awe for it's purposes. It was pointed out to me lately that the ex-chancellor Nigel Lawson said Shakespeare was a tory because of the law-and-order speeches in *Troilus and Cressida*. The speeches are there - but the play ruthlessly destroys them and their arguments in the course of the story. Lawson venerates the text because of something it says. He hasnt been taught how to read the text properly. It argues against the values of toryism.

I can only make sense of the human mind - and how authority may turn it against itself - by understanding what imagination is. That it is the child's necessary first map of the world - the child must always imagine, interpret, beyond the possible limits of it's understanding. Yet the map must be complete, must accommodate everything - even what is mysterious. This map is partly factual, partly purely fanciful - that the factual needs the fanciful is what stops fancy being arbitrary and raises it to the reality of imagination. But all future maps must be written over the first map - in palimpsest, and reincorporate (often) the tracings of the past. Imagination (for the young) often supplies meaning (or at any rate interpretation) to matters that are really conventional (such as the role assigned to a god) and cannot be reduced to fact. Even the adult mind is in many areas as factually ignorant as the child's. These areas are often of great importance - and uncatered for by instinct simply because they are produced by a post-instinctual society. They "justify" the facts: and so fact can never be divorced from value, emotion and total meaning. Total meaning is really imagination. Imagination is both knowledge and the need to know: it is not idle curiosity but curiosity based on the need to contextualise what is already known and thus to extend it. Two elements then become important. How is imagination developed and later used? If it is constantly disciplined by the facts-of-the-world then it becomes profounded. The facts do not sterilize imagination - making it more profound and human (if I can throw in those words for the moment). Facts should always evoke imagination, the contextualising ability, not sterilize it. But you can see that the imagination can become a function into which more and more falsehoods, ideological figments, will be inseminated. Ideology works on the assumption that ignorance is the adult's birthright. In the education of the young there is a point or period where the imagination can either assert itself - and the child becomes autonomous: or authority occupies the imagination - and the individual ceases to be itself and becomes a projection of authority's purposes. (Authority is the power owned by the ruling class: and so it comes about that democracy is merely another way in which people are owned - this time through ideological possession.) Imagination isnt - even when its autonomous - a solace, a fanciful rectification of metaphysical discomforts. Imagination may often be confrontation with the tragic: an inability to bear the tragic means that you are ideologically owned, that you have no self but are merely a walking state embodiment. Of course authority is amply sufficient at using awe and wonderment for its own ideological purposes. That is the danger. A sense of awe and wonderment may very easily be a weakness - it depends on the individual's imaginative autonomy. I've yet to see a TV advertisement that advertises a tragic experience as a commodity... A child that never wept would be inhuman: an adult without a sense of tragedy is inhuman.

Above I referred to two important elements. I have been talking of the first. The second is harder to talk about. It is the element of value: all values are imaginary, no one decrees values like a divine mint issuing notes of value. Values are what people have created as they became aware of their situation. In the end I think the only value is: I have a right to know. The right has been established in a non-moral, utilitarian way. If I cannot know I cannot function: I become autistic, either clinically or morally. The latter is non-utilitarian because it means I cannot make prudential distinctions. I may use my moral blindness to exploit others and become rich. Of course, such a person would probably not be cynical, but on the contrary self-righteous: because he would understand himself ideologically... But societies are formally egalitarian and moral-blindness is total, so if I am morally-blind I am likely to break the law as well as bend it to my use; and also other social infringements may follow, the rich are often unable to enjoy their riches, cut off from others, they are miserly, neurotic and so on. But I wont pursue this point. My point is that imagination is founded on - is psychically the product of - the right to know and therefore to be (the two go together). But this means according the rights of others to be - which is really a paradox or contradiction, because conceding this infringes your own rights. You must share the world: the idea is so fraught that people have preferred to share it with god rather than with each other. It is difficult for the child to learn this act of sharing by which the child in fact creates itself: there are others - and there is itself. It isnt a matter of sharing your toys or sweets... It is profoundly philosophical, a crisis, because it means sharing the *world* - and once the garment is rent, it means recognizing death. To recognize others means to learn about your own death: that is tragic, but it is also the only possible basis of happiness and democracy. When authority makes imagination ideological it diverts this process. Instead of imagination increasingly sharing itself - accepting that sort of existential responsibility - it ceases to develop at all, it ceases to be itself. Imagination, in reaction, has become not the origin of conscious human life, but its death. The reactionary carry their dead selves within them. That is the aim of authoritarian education: to make the child pregnant with death. For any individual, the death of the self means the death of others. Even the beloved Leader is really hated... Humanly, the imagination which recognizes and expresses its right to live becomes the same right of others. Inhumanly, imagination becomes a basis of repression: of the self and others - doctrines of original sin, socio-biological doctrines of the necessary animality of human beings, political doctrines of racial and class superiority and cultures based on this.

At the base of the value there seems to be a fact. If value is an assertion of the imagination, then the right to be is a fact for the imagination which is being. Yet the imagination is the necessary action of apprehending, situating after recognizing, facts: so the imagination must establish its right as a fact. For what this argument is worth! But I would like you to see how imagination and fact must always create each other if the individual is to be human, to create and recreate humanity as the known facts change and are changed by the individuals and their society and technology.

Imagination has its proper education. Part of this is the whole dramatic and poetic experience. Imagination is also the basis of the distinction between reaction and revolution, between the retrogressive and the progressive. Its what makes someone a tory or a socialist, robotized by the state or freed into socialist consciousness, with its tragedy, with the only possibility (which it gives) of a better and more humane world. Our minds are like our bodies, are soft malleable creations in a hard, factual, objective world. Imagination is what makes it necessary and possible for us to change the world - because it is the source of practical need and desire and value. It also creates the possibility that we will become the walking dead who will destroy the world. But imagination cannot be adequately summarized under words such as awe and wonder: because imagination makes action necessary, it expresses imagination and makes imagination possible. Imagination is the process of action to embody value in the valueless universe. Awe and wonder are often only ideological desensitization.

This is what makes drama important. Because the imagination is necessarily a drama-creating process. Drama can be used to encourage and confront the imagination so that it asserts its need for value in a way in which it must be responsible for itself: it must experience the creation of what is imagined. But ideology presents the created image whole, emblematically as this or that, and the reactionary reacts accordingly. The reactionary becomes a victim not a creator. Socialism needs drama - and not merely in the reduced form of social realism. This had some point when it was used to de-mystify art of its ideological subterfuges, the use made of its old authoritarian powers: but inevitably the process goes too far, and social-realism itself becomes reductive. I say inevitably, because the new authority is trying to do what can only be done in the drama of the imaginative mind. Then instead of the party wanting to lead, it wants to *be* the others... In future the success of revolution will be measured - it will be a cause and a sign - by the profundity of its drama and the extent of its audiences. Art does not replace political action, preempt it or even have authority over it; but without it the progressive becomes the retrogressive.

What teachers do is of great importance. And it is important that they become crystal clear about what they are doing and about its consequences. Otherwise with the best of intentions, they will serve reaction.

Yours sincerely,

Edward Bond

Chapter Four

Productions

Ian Stuart

London   23 March 1985

Dear Ian Stuart,

You make a distinction between the "vital action of the argument" and other, perhaps less important but more involving aspects of a play. I dont make a distinction between these two things. I pursue an argument, but this isnt verbal or cerebral only. I use reason and also emotion. Climaxes are verbal - and to do with radical or revealing ideas - as well as emotional and dramatic in a more conventional sense. Often when my characters are under greatest emotional stress they produce a new idea. It's usually assumed that emotional responses are biologically fixed. And bad dramatic writing is based on this assumption. But in fact emotions are socially based - and are a combination of convention and necessity (thus there is an etiquette of eating which is also an essential activity: if you get your table manners wrong you appear like an animal - your biological status is altered!). What happens in my plays (often to the confusion of critics) is that I realign emotion and reason to produce a rational survey of the events I'm using. This is a poetic process and you cant have epic without poetry.

Why is it that the Greeks and Shakespeare used poetry for their characters - and that Ibsen and Chekov also needed it in their more prosaic time? Ultimately this is because history moves through individual psychology - and poetry is the social in the human being (not the private soul sheltering egoistically from the social). Poetry is the social nature of the human being, in it what is most personal is shared with other humans. This is access to the process by which human beings create themselves, producing their subjectivity in response to historical movement. This is a subjective process necessary to social living and so all humans live in a poetic relation with the mundane - even if this is repressed by a vulgarization of culture. Poetry, as used by a dramatist, isnt therefore a heightened language which the dramatist forces onto experience - it is the language of ordinary daily reality. But the dramatist changes the "substance" of poetry by infiltrating it with new ideas. His ideas are rational analyses of historical, social movements: they explain the individual and the social in terms of each other. So a dramatic process needs to be a unity, and cant be split up in the way you suggest. My advantage is that I "automatically" write from a class-view which now has historical initiative. Im not reluctant about boasting this. After all they used to say it was something to be proud of if you went to a good school. I happen to come from the class of contemporary historical initiative. This made things hard for me when I first started to write - since the institutions and conventions of writing were owned by other classes: but now that I've been able to surmount the preliminary hurdles, my background becomes an advantage - and I watch with sympathy the struggles of the writers, such as David Hare, who didnt have all my advantages...

I dont worry about what Irving Wardle says. I am an optimist because social change is to my advantage. To Yeats, Bloomsburyites and most drama critics change means de-culture, a collapse of privileged values. You could scrawl my lines in chalk on the street and they'd make sense (or as much sense as they make on the page). The lines of a Bloomsbury poet would not be so at home. There is a line in my poem "Advice to Actors": The pessimism of one man and the optimism of his neighbour/ May change the world in the same way. If Im concerned with the change of power necessary to maintain and develop culture, then those who now have cultural power must view my work pessimistically. Their judgement on my work is necessarily a judgement on their lives. The final arbitration is the judgement made by political developments. Bloomsburyism must lead to barbarisms in a changing world. That's why Schiller was studied by the commandants of death-camps. I've tried to explain this in my paper "The Basis of Material Aesthetics" which will be the introduction to the 3rd volume of my collected plays: this will be published later this year.[1]

I wouldnt write my early plays now because I've developed a more refined

---

[1] *Bond Plays:Three* London: Methuen, 1987 was published with a different introduction.

analytic dramaturgy - so I can analyse deeper. Some of the audience would rather extend sympathy than understanding (it's better to give charity than to need to receive it). But I havent altered my political or social purpose. All the great discoveries in science are made through loopholes, or built out of flaws. There are no doorways in truths, instead there are cracks. Where the theory doesnt work, where the model doesnt fit, there is the access to the new theory, the improved model. I suppose people want drama to complete their living for them, to be an alternative to it. And it's true that the dramatic experience is part of life, not a relaxation from it - an element in life as much eating is. Yet it cannot be a substitute - it gives experiences which have to become social skills, social knowledge, and therefore part of the extradramatic life of the audience. So I think that what I have to do is provide "elements" (facts, incidents) which are unavoidable, and which the audience have to come to terms with: I dramatise their ordinary daily life outside the theatre by putting a new element into it. I set them a new question and point out in them the means they can muster to answer it. This often means looking at difficult and dangerous areas of experience, areas in which a great deal of cultural-definition is invested. I need show only one twitch under the coat to show that whatever wears it is living, one movement inside the atom to show it isnt an ultimate frontier. Then the psyche and practice of the audience are activated - and they must reidentify themselves, by change which is either conformation or reaction.

I dislike the present production of *Saved*.[2] The actors dont know what they're doing. They in fact told me so. A few days before he began rehearsals the director told me that present day young writers couldnt deal with "whole" social problems but only with small areas of experience. This is perhaps true of the whole of theatre and not only of writers. I'll try to explain. The original productions of *Pope's Wedding* and *Saved* were better than the revivals. This isnt the enhancement of retrospect. Im too accurate an observer of my work to be confused about that. Yet the present actors and directors were better placed to do the plays. To begin with, the present day actors are more serious. Twenty years ago it wasnt the thing to take yourself too seriously - that was left to method actors. Now society is much more "performance" conscious and so theatre-workers take themselves more seriously. They're also much less naive, they have

---

[2] The production of *Saved*, directed by Danny Boyle, was in a double-bill with *The Pope's Wedding*, directed by Max Stafford-Clark, Royal Court Theatre, 1985.

"seen through" more, are not so easily morally blackmailed as people were twenty years ago. This is true of all or certainly most young people. Punks are politically more radical (especially psychologically) than socialists twenty years ago. Yet their radicalism is critical rather than creative. They have no conceptual politics in which to place it. They inherit the failure of the sixties. I didnt believe in the sixties as a political movement, though I enjoyed its psychological escape from conservative-conformity. Punks are often politically radical in a way more advanced than "beautiful people" of twenty years ago. Oddly what happens in the theatre with the new seriousness is a return to naturalism - and an avoidance of the epic. What should be epic merely becomes grandiose or surreal. It lacks the basis in naturalism. Naturalism combines with poetry/epic - this produces realism, which is my sort of theatre. What happens with the present productions of *S* and *PW* is that the realism gets reduced to naturalism, the poetry is removed and with it the epic analysis. *PW* is closer to naturalism than *S*, so *PW* works better as naturalism. Even so, the director wanted to cut the tins at the end, he wanted to cut the scene with the cup - and the radical reassessment of the activity of laying the table (using the teapot, food etc.) which precedes it. So psychology was being removed from history. Another example: the throwing of stones is as important in *PW* as in *Saved*. It's essential that the throwing of the stones in the pond should be an event of beauty to the actors and the audience. To stop this being sentimental (I noticed how) the play ruthlessly precedes the moment by repeating the word piss! (Also a denigration of the moonlit water of the pond.) Yet the production ignores the value of this moment (even though I've asked for it to be looked at). Later when the stones are thrown against the hut we should see the violence not as an animal expression but as related to a moment of beauty, a time when people wished to recreate their lives. That's what I mean by epic poetry. (I need hardly point out that the stones are used again in *Saved*....) Note also that in the little scene of the group before the house is attacked the epic game of cricket becomes the commercialised sport of the boxing match. Actors and directors have to be aware of the structures the dramatist is using to co-operate in an experience with the audience - out of which the dramatic learning will come. (I could point out how much of *Macbeth* is built on the image of a gate, and how this image is repeated in fantastic variations: gatekeeper, cauldron as gate, caesarian birth as being avoidance of gate till the gate comes to get him! - the dark wood, which (as Dante understood) was a gate.) You can reduce any good play to units of about seven lines. These units will repeat and repeat the basic dramaturgy of the play, and the whole play will be found in each of them (thus you could look for the gate unit in *Macbeth*) - and they combine to create the experience and learning of the whole play: Shakespeare will have to put a name on the door over the gate at the end. Now this process isnt understood in the present day theatre, by writers or others. That's its limitation: it avoids the poetic and thus the epic, and so it removes conceptualization from experience, extracts history from psychology. And because this means there's no dramatic substance in the work, external theories have to be introduced. Thus the gangs are explained in sociobiological terms. I found that during the stoning of the baby all the actors were going through method-like interiorized dramatizations of their motives. Im throwing this stone because he threw that one and Im in a power-ploy situation with him... This conveyed nothing to the audience. You cant reduce my plays to this sort of explanation any more than you can reduce the Sistine Chapel to theology. It's true that I use power-relation within the group, but my real questions are different. Why, for example, are their power relations? Why build the chapel roof? (Not as a canvas for Michelangelo - ultimately he is describing the process of building the roof not decorating it.) When I was told the *PW* was being rehearsed in an Essex village I said they should rehearse it on an oil rig. I meant this. I was told that they'd actually met a "hermit" in this village. I asked them if they'd seen any corpses. (They could have seen these among the tins in the Kings Road supermarket - but they went unnoticed.)

What is lacking in the theatre are dramatic tools. And this corresponds to a lack outside the theatre: radical analysis. The sixties (and earlier) analyses of politics and psychology are seen to be inadequate. Socialism is conceived to be a human desire the naivety of which becomes wrecked on the rocks of real politics. I dont believe this. We have to understand that history and psychology are both mutually creating, so that human beings can only be understood politically. But it isnt a matter of sloughing of social deformations to get to the real human reality beneath them. The capacities - emotional, dynamic, intellectual - of human beings are neutral - there is no pure state - and we have to understand the process of creation. This isnt arbitrary, as Brecht seems to suggest in *Man is Man* - there is a political necessity. Again Ive tried to describe this in "The Basis of Material Aesthetics." Unfortunately I dont know of any theatre where these problems are understood. At the moment what happens at the Royal Court is SDP liberalism. It not a radical questioning and recreation of human experience. In fact, the psychological forms on the street are more advanced than those used in the theatre. In the theatre they're liberalism tempered with dissident enlightenment. I found that the interpretation of psychology in *Saved* wasnt twenty years behind the present Court work but still in advance of it. Unfortunately the theatre has become a more enclosed world. The directors now write the plays with the writer. The idea of the writer writing them with the street (as it were) doesnt exist for them. The danger they wish to escape from is the idea that the writer writes with his soul. But does anyone seriously believe that anymore? The writer is someone with a skill that relates him in a special way to the world outside the theatre. He is the bridge to the stage. Of course, directors could function *also* as writers. But in practice they're not. They write, put together, plays like directors not writers. And so they and the actors are not set the fundamental radical problems: instead they're solved aesthetically "inside the theatre." Yet aesthetics must be the means by which the street is conveyed into the theatre - because people in the street are in a radical aesthetic element; it is produced in the daily activity of maintaining life, in relations with the self (morality, happiness etc) and the city - work, social conduct etc. The result is that young writers arent being allowed to learn a dramatic-craft - I mean by that an efficient means of conveying information on the stage, and so they dont know what they can bring onto the stage. That is the present situation.

In a nutshell, the dramatist must pursue the street, but what happened in *PW* and *S* at the Court is the director pursuing his own end: yet a play is a specific instrument. You can use a surgeon's knife to peel an apple, but it wont help the patient.

Yours sincerely,

Edward Bond

Adrian Noble
Royal Shakespeare Company
London EC2   24 September 1988

Dear Adrian,

Thanks for your letter. Im glad *Restoration* went well. I've read some of the critics. Really they hate my guts with all their hearts... but are afraid to say so. The only one I respected was the one in the *Sunday Times*: a dog should bark and not miaow. I'll certainly make a point of seeing the production.

Im really very grateful for the RSC productions of my plays - it's about five by now. The RSC is the only British theatre that pays much attention to my plays. I'd disappear (in England) without it. Thats what I *would* most like to do - disappear and write quietly. I used to wonder how Schubert could bear to write and not hear what he'd written. Now Im older I see that doesnt matter - the point is to write. To make sure it goes onto paper and to assume that in time it would be useful. A hundred years from now I would like to be able to walk down a street and - seeing a woman who'd dropped her shopping - help her chase the oranges and apples and rolls and put them back into her shopping bag. I wont be able to do that or anything as interesting - but perhaps at least one of her relatives might see one of my plays and understand it: that would be second best to helping with the shopping but better than nothing. There is the problem of whether there will still be any streets or any oranges - and it's for this one writes. Not to be admired or venerated in any way by posterity! - but so that it may drop its shopping in the street.

I've been reading Gaskill's book.[1] It's very interesting - he has faults but they seem to damage him rather than others. I owe very much to him. He says that writers need to be connected to a theatre. That's true - and I had the fortune to be connected with the Court when I was developing. I dont think he liked a lot of what I wrote even then - but if that's what I needed to write, that's what he'd do... as long as he could. I feel his current criticism of me doesnt touch me. I think I can combine what he admires with other things he cant understand. I dont think he's developed, because he cut the umbilical cord - and curiously in the theatre it's the children who feed the mothers. Since the Court I havent had a

---

[1] *A Sense of Direction* by William Gaskill, London: Faber & Faber, 1989.

"home theatre" and this has been a difficulty for me. A writer needs to cross different terrains in order to get anywhere. You need Timon as well as Lear, Pericles as well as Cymbeline - without the lesser plays you dont know how to do the other plays. I mean technically how: you learn how to do Cymbeline from doing Pericles - and then the wonderful innovatory craftsmanship of Cymbeline becomes clear. Writers need it - so do directors and audiences. The West works on a success ethic and so misvalues - and so misunderstands. When I sent *The Worlds* to the RSC someone decided they didnt like it, they wouldnt do. That's a mistake - you produce the writer not the play (because the writer produces the street and you cant knock gaps into a street). Only prostitutes are expected to be good every time. Of course if the writer goes gaga or starts producing rubbish, that's another thing. But *The Worlds* is an exciting - rather impertinent - play: and there's a great deal of theatrical craft in it: craft instruments designed to deliver the present day. Writers dont bring methods of interpretation to their subjects, they learn them from their subjects: the subjects teach method. And I think perhaps that *is* a stage to which the writer has access which others dont - it's because he or she needs that stage in order to analyse what is previously unanalysed. When I saw *Pope's Wedding* revived at the Court I was amazed at how much I knew about theatre... and not conscious of where I'd learned it.[2] But obviously I had learned it. Yet Devine could see no stagecraft in *Saved* or *Pope's Wedding* (wouldnt hold the stage he told me). This is because I was adapting method to new ends - and he made it possible for me to do so and after him Gaskill did. (Then Devine died and Gaskill went into Joint Stock.) I learned stagecraft from an urgent necessity to understand the street and by watching how other dramatists dealt with it - some ancient, others modern. I feel young writers dont have a chance to see what modern stagecraft could be - how a truth invents its own movements - and how urgency creates it own recollection. Younger writers can only learn this from older writers - of whom Im now one. It's not that younger writers need to copy older writers. They need to be accurately challenged - or accurately (not slovenly or incompetently) disappointed or frustrated by them. Audiences need this too. Audiences have to learn the craft of theatre-going - the craft of being shocked in the theatre if necessary, but not wilfully shocked - shocked by reason and necessity.

    I had some relationship with Howard Davies. But he ducked out on *The*

---

[2] Bond refers to the production of *The Pope's Wedding* directed by Max Stafford-Clark, Royal Court Theatre, 1985.

Worlds and I think his work has become empty. He needed that stage of development as much as I did. His *Mother Courage* was in many ways excellent (ignoring the mess up with the machinery and the inaudibility and the silly music - but these are incidentals). What he missed - and made the production work in such a way that what was missing wasnt noticed - was the whole point of the play. Really what he did is what most theatre knows how to do - it has reduced the method to the treatment: the philosophy is essentially sociobiological. It gets confused with things like the circus (will Katrina actually fall off so high a roof?... the Berliner Ensemble made the roof so low the officer could have pulled her off it: yet the scene was tenser than it was at the Barbican, and the vista was enormous - depths and heights greater than any stage roof). How has replaced why. Can you imagine Chaplin or a clown actually dying - at a circus? (It would be an accident - at the circus.) Chaplin didnt have the art (you've seen his *Hamlet* snippet?). There is a reality about the stage which isnt available to the circus. The circus is too real in that it faces us with our nightmares. In the theatre we stand behind our nightmares or dreams: we watch the actors from the front - but stand behind them. In the circus you are too menaced to stand behind the clown: he confronts you. But when you go behind the actor you share something universal - a community. The circus confronts you, the theatre makes you social - you understand the sufferings and happinesses of a common humanity. That's what the Berliner Ensemble's *Mother C.* gave - and Howard Davies couldnt. What? - because he hadnt done *The Worlds*?... Well no, not exactly. But because he'd mistaken the process, and you can only learn that in relation to your own time, your own society. We cannot tell the time by looking at the clock face, we have to take the clock to pieces to find the time in it. If you confuse the two you make things work - but at a great cost. You can still do a stirring job on Brecht and cook something up: but I dont think you can do this on a modern play. There has been a radical change in the functioning of human consciousness since Brecht: the audience's minds work differently. They will still respond to previous patterns of working - but again only at that cost.

I'll try to explain. It has to do with the business of where we get a sense of value from. The first stories were told by animals and natural elements to men - these are the religious stories of totems and natural forces, the anthropomorphic world. As societies became more ordered and hierarchic stories were told by gods to men: as before, the values were *imposed*, this time by gods, the meaning *was* the gods' - and if it was obscure the only possible stance for men was acceptance and adaptation. The whole of classical philosophy is about that. The Christian story is told by one god not a chorus of gods: that means blood, because God comes closer. So the stories of the Christian era - told by God to believers - are to do with suffering, martyrdoms, and miracles. The Renaissance is based on stories told by the devil to men: Iago is a devil in so far as he does not refer to any force outside himself. Milton, Goethe, Blake all tell devil stories in various ways. This is because force is being released in the industrialised earth. In *Restoration* its coal underground not the devil - and as the play comes to its end Are has to become satanic in order to express a new power. Miracles become irrelevant: a god might make a beggar girl see, but would he repair a power station? And the devil has his own martyrdoms - wars and holocausts of martyrdoms. So who tells the stories now? First, the uncreative stories are told by the advertising agencies and in their stronghold on Broadway. To a limited extent the stories can be infiltrated in other ways, but only limitedly. The *creative* story is something different: for the first time in human history men and women tell stories to men and women. No animals, deities, no natural forces, no gods, no devils - us. That is new - it made Dostoevski a fanatic, Tolstoy an evader (the letters to the Tsar are pure self-delusion) and Nietzsche mad. Because where does the value come from - how to even analyse sufficiently to describe, let alone to judge - it seems a world beyond good and evil, yet full of disasters and even successes trailing disasters behind them. No doubt it's a temporary stage, but for the first time the end of the story no longer can make sense of the stages of the story: which is what has always so far been the case in art. It's now the case that the stages of the story must make sense of the end - I put it crudely because there still has to be concordance between the two. But it means that the "incident" has to be exposed in new ways. I arrive at this not theoretically, but through the need to record the street. By-roads open to Brecht and others before him arent open to us. Human beings create value - and yet they need value in order to describe themselves in art. It seems circular - but the solution is always in where the stress, strain, breakage, is placed. Godot creates a void - doesnt come (the boy's descriptions of face-to-face encounters with Godot are amazingly sentimental, off a Victorian Christmas card). Chaplin cant show the death of the clown (though he can make him a murderer). The void is the ash pit of concentration camps. It has to be filled by a new description of "being human." That's the function of art. The crisis we're living through is about that. Punks dressed as devils - why not angels? They could've pinned up halos and put on little wings? It is a crisis of value and so of description. *Human Cannon* is mostly a study of goodness - when the good woman prostitutes her daughter, kills a soldier who might be her son - and kills others who're normally excusable through ignorance - and then has the soldier run on with his trousers in the farce position: I confess Im not sure what the author is asking of me. Fortunately there is an act to follow. The play works - because I've seen it. But it's not going to be done as Howard Davies would have done it. I dont mind treading on toes or even spitting in faces - but I wont spit into the void. It would make my life meaningless. *Company of Men* is a study in evil. If you want a classical precedent, think of *Macbeth*. Everything is told two or three times - but no Beckett's absurdist twice: - gabble it the second time (as he recommended). The men in *Company of Men* go into cellars and even deep into submarines in order to find truths which perhaps they dont recognise? - and Macbeth must summon the wood to his castle. Perhaps a new way of speaking is required for the characters - an invented form of whispering? - a fluent stuttering? - various other approaches. (The game for *The Worlds* is to let the chess pieces speak their roles in the game. An intellectual pleasure - if you want a classical model for *The Worlds*, it's Moliere.)

You see the sort of problem Im trying to deal with. If I can share the problems creatively with others Id be happy to do so. If the worse came to the worse, penury might force my hand... but it would be a loss I'd do almost everything to avoid. I take my writing seriously because I grew up in a war. I remember the terror of being bombed and bombed and bombed. I think it created a great grave inside me - and I have learned the joy of living resurrections. My plays are a series of resurrections. To go back to Gaskill, it would be very easy to give Len fist clenching gestures at the end of *Saved* - how could that be a problem? But I remember I thought that wasnt necessary, since the character was then sure: he held the play in his hand as it were. Strength and joy were dehumanised by the Nazis: the problem is to describe these things humanely. People telling stories to people. An epic theatre.

I've tried many ways to relate to the present theatre. I dont interfere with rehearsals of revivals - and Im adaptable. But I wont get into the position I did over the *War Plays*. *Great Peace* is the best play I've written - when the woman goes away at the end in order to become the foundation of the new city I achieved the sort of thing a lot of theatre has searched for. It's said: hold a mirror up to nature. We can also say: hold a camera to the face close enough to see society in it. The *War Plays* have a development from agit prop to another sort of theatre where there is a camera on stage which is not seen because now it's in the audience's eyes (they cant get rid of it, as Oedipus did) and we have to bring it close to the face in order to see everything else: that's modern agit prop - bringing the camera close to the face so that society can be seen in it - moving camera not static mirror.

Anyway I have my problems and I can wait. But if you want to come and talk to me about them, I'd always be happy to see you. You lost some of my confidence when you were so convinced about throwing me over in order to keep Di Travis (and Im truely glad she didnt do it, by the way).[3] But I suppose you were under pressure at the time and you did sound sad or at any rate distracted. You could always get Howard Davies back to do the *Glass Menagerie*?

Best wishes,

Edward Bond

---

[3] Adrian Noble wanted Di Travis to direct the RSC's revival of *Restoration* which opened at the Swan Theatre, Stratford-upon-Avon, 13 September, 1988.

David Jansen
Willowdale, Ontario
Canada   3 October 1989

Dear David,

Thanks for your letter and for the two papers.[1]

Anna Massey's remark that I didn't want to show any goodness in Xenia: this should be commented upon because it shows very accurately the sort of difficulties that have to be coped with.[2] The text makes a great point of saying that there is too much good in Xenia. Unfortunately, Xenia doesn't believe this and so can't make her goodness productive and act on it: that is why she is a ghost and why she becomes destructive. We need to show how the dead wound themselves (it's their way of keeping a toe-hold on life). Lady Macbeth must walk in a certain way in order to keep the candle alight (in the sleep walking scene). Her walking invokes the walk of the ghost in the banqueting scene. Yet she takes great care to keep the little flame alight: she is an image of creativity. She rubs her hands while carrying the taper. The murderess has become the image of creativity - but there is a lingering franticness in the writhing hands. These are very subtle ways of showing "goodness." But what conventional actresses want to do is show a conventional watering down of goodness - so that really to be good is to be crippled, though they think this is ennobling their character, making it interesting, showing it in the round, etc. I do not want to show Xenia as evil - like some political fanatic who wants to label his enemies all the time. When Nazi concentration camp guards read their Christmas cards, were they good? How do you read Christmas cards in a concentration camp? Now you could say "Well, under it all, the guard was a good man, and what a pity it all is, and if only... etc., etc." All of this seems to me trite. Xenia sells and wears beautiful clothes because she wishes to disguise her own death. If you like, Xenia was killed when she went to the island to rescue Marthe. We need to explore the various stages of Xenia's deadness - and how she disguises it from herself. I wasn't able to interest Anna Massey in these things. Her approach is made clear

---

[1] The paper Bond subsequently refers to is David Jansen's "Working from 'Up Here,'" unpublished dissertation, Royal Holloway and Bedford New College, May, 1989.

[2] Anna Massey played Xenia in *Summer* in the Cottesloe at the National Theatre, 27 January - 19 June, 1982. Massey's remarks are to be found in Jansen's dissertation.

in the following incident.

She said she knew how to play her scenes with Marthe. They would each stand on one side of the stage and bat the lines to each other, as in tennis. This is, in fact, a possible solution, if it is arrived at analytically and is supported by the rest of the performances (of other scenes): because the sort of "batting" would then be defined. But she meant it as a technical solution. Really, this isn't acting at all. It's delivering.

When an outside director comes to one of the big theatres, especially if he is not part of the touring circus, he gets involved (even though he doesn't take part) in that theatre's squabbles: he has gone into the ghetto. Susan Fleetwood was, when I directed *The Woman*, friendly with the man Hall wanted to co-direct with me: I didn't want to co-direct with him because he was more at home with the theatre of, say, Anna Massey.[3] In the end, I gave an ultimatum to Hall that either the other director went or I did. Hall made his decision. Susan Fleetwood strongly objected to this and during the play rehearsals was obstructive and resentful: for example she quarrelled with Bryceland. Naturally Fleetwood polarised some of the cast. All this is very silly and a waste. But it does have its effect. I had brought Bryceland in from outside the company (against Peter Hall's wishes).

About the RSC and *War Plays*. You should make it clear that I left the production.[4] I found the work frustrating and I thought the actors were being self-defeating. I'd decided to co-direct the play with a younger director. I wanted to try to understand what a new younger theatre was about. Actually I found that it was about being lost. I'd also hoped that having a house director would solve some of the administrative problems for me. It didnt and I found that I was asked to attend meetings to "give weight" to our case. I found that the younger director was involved in questions about "how to make it work" - it's much the situation that cropped up with the RSC production of *Restoration* (when I didnt attend rehearsals).[5] Ian McDiarmid was a special problem.[6] He was quarrelling with

---

[3] Bond made his directorial debut with *The Woman* in the Olivier, National Theatre, 10 August, 1978. Peter Hall was the Artistic Director of the National Theatre from 1972 to 1987.

[4] *The War Plays* consist of three separate plays: *Red Black and Ignorant, The Tin Can People* and *Great Peace*. The first two parts opened in the Pit at the Barbican Centre on 29 May, 1985 with *Great Peace* joining the repertoire on 17 July, 1985. *The War Plays* were directed by Edward Bond and Nick Hamm. Bond left rehearsals at the end of May, 1985.

[5] The Royal Shakespeare Company produced *Restoration* in the Swan Theatre, Stratford-upon-Avon, directed by Roger Michell. The production opened on 13 September, 1988. Bond subsequently re-rehearsed sections of the play prior to its opening at the Pit, Barbican Centre,

the theatre - he'd written a letter to a newspaper attacking the RSC directors (or certainly one of them). He was concerned with the role of the actor as director (a movement that was then prominent in the British theatre) and subsequently went on to run a theatre. He was cast as the main part in the middle play without my knowledge or permission. The part is for a young actor - he represents the ancient corn god born each spring: McDiarmid is late forties and looks it (or he might be fifties). The casting was absurd - it was like asking a geriatric to play Romeo. I was told that I had to have him because the situation in the theatre was so tense that if I said "no" all the actors would go on strike. After I'd learned more about the other actors I knew this not to be so. But at the time I accepted the casting. Of course I shouldnt have: but it would after all be interesting to get a geriatric to play Romeo...? I suppose I was tempted by the challenge. In fact McDiarmid played the part well - but not as my character and not in my play. He produced a sort of Beckett eccentric. But I suppose an aging actor playing Romeo cant have a good time. Im sure that on one level McDiarmid knew he was wrongly cast. He had to act very athletically in the penultimate scene - jumping about to save his life. Inevitably he sprained his ankle. So for many performances a stunt man had to come on at a certain moment and take over the part - while McDiarmid stood on stage. It was wonderful. It was as if the real spirit of the character was suddenly released onto the stage - history came alive. Unfortunately McDiarmid got better and the stunt man had to go.

Im told that in a recent book Max Stafford-Clark says I get too close to the play when I direct. He watched me direct one afternoon. Afterwards he said "very interesting but you do too much of the work." I had four weeks to direct a complicated play and get the music composed and learned. I had to get close and do more than I would have chosen. Stafford-Clark took six months to work on his next production. He did it a la Joint Stock so the play was also written at that time. But rehearsals began on day one of six months. So of course actors have time to think and develop and be more creative. Someone who runs a theatre should acknowledge the difference between six months and one month. Max Stafford-Clark's play was pretty much a flop - and the writer involved in it said he didnt like doing it. *Restoration* was one of the Court's biggest successes at that

---

London, on 29 March, 1989.

6 In the 1985 RSC production Ian McDiarmid appeared as the Monster in *Red Black and Ignorant*, the First Man in *The Tin Can People*, the Officer and Middle Aged Man in *Great Peace*.

time - though it was badly underrehearsed. What can one do? I feel our whole theatre is at the moment moribund - and really this comes from the people who run the theatres.

I've now decided that I'll work in them only when I can get proper conditions and when theatres need me. Max Stafford-Clark has run the Court for ten years or so and really done very little. The RSC is a vulgar mess. And the NT is still recovering from the heady days of *Amadeus* and *Guys and Dolls*. None of the directors of these theatres has found a way of getting a new theatre onto the stages: I dont mean just plays, I mean a theatre that escapes the profit-performance scourge of technological-capitalist society: to get to process instead of products; processes are created, products consumed. When Howard Davies says I try to change acting all at once, I must answer that that's the only chance I have; really he's saying something as unconsidered as Max Stafford-Clark. I think they're, instead of changing, wasting their chances and their lives: and I point to the static nature of what they do as evidence. But, and this is my most important personal point, he's wrong to say Im angry. That doesnt help. I am not angry because I am far too interested in what Im doing. They go on with their revivals and their manipulations of younger writers. The bad thing for me is that in a way it's tempting to have less and less to do with them: because I can go on writing, because I can go on being involved in the theatre of life outside the theatre. These are extraordinary times in which to write.

And now I'll try to answer some of your other points. Im writing an introduction on Postmodernism for *Jackets* and *Company of Men*. They're being published next spring together with a short play called *September*, which was performed about a week ago in Canterbury Cathedral.[7] It's about the murder of Chico Mendes. I didnt go to rehearsals or see the production... I cant let you have the introduction yet because Im working on it still. I call the book "postmodern" as a challenge to the usual use of these words. We live in a postmodern world and it would be absurd to go through the political motions of the past. Instead P[ost] M[odernism] is usually a return to a reactionary classicism: the solid architecture that appears in Chico's dreams, nobility and angst? There is also a return to early Brecht as if by avoiding his politics you avoided mistakes: the theatre of Heinrich Müller and Robert Wilson. I want a theatre of immediate political involvement - but not one of propaganda for

---

[7] *September* was performed in Canterbury Cathedral on 16 September, 1989.

propaganda's sake (which is what propaganda is if it anticipates revolution). Curiously we have to tell people not how to make bread (or cars) but that they are hungry and tired - and have a right to be these things: that is how to recreate our and their energy. We need to contact the processes by which people create themselves and then art becomes action. This is very vaguely put but I'll try to make it clearer in the introduction to the book.

And lastly your question about political violence. How do we know what the ultimate terminus of any violence will be? I accept that we dont. Violence should always be avoided if humanly possible. But there are two questions. One, what creates violence. And two, what legitimizes it. American society is violent and this violence (since it isnt so prevalent in other societies) is either a result of the sort of people Americans are or the sort of society they have. You could say that through immigration America has attracted a certain sort of people. But I dont believe that - it is truly a melting pot, though the ingredients havent necessarily yet melted. So I think American society creates violence. If you have say churches preaching against violence these in fact become institutions of violence - religion becomes a form of aggression; for example it often insists on nuclear weapons, this creates an atmosphere of repression and danger from the top, and this spirals down into cultural, street violence. Postmodernism is a society of wants not needs. I know of course that many people in these societies are still in need. But like the starving in Africa, the cultural horizon of their death isnt that no one comes with a piece of bread and a cup of water, but that they havent got helicopters, power stations, tractors, reservoirs, etc. - in other words they know they die from lack of luxuries: only if your society has the luxuries (the wants) can you meet the needs. It seems that a society of wants is necessarily a society of terrors: the great technology goes wrong, it breaks down and even when it works it can be destructive. The society of needs knew destitution. The society of wants lives in terror. And is therefore violent. It also, of course, creates terrorism - which is the relation it creates with the old societies of needs (and the culture of these societies can survive into the new culture). The postmodern world is for these reasons violent. The progressive idea earlier in the last two centuries or so was that if technology could solve economic problems the world would be freed from its ancient miseries: Postmodernism recreates those miseries. Affluence - technological brilliance - doesnt dispose of politics. We are still left with the basic choice: fascism or socialism. Current events shouldnt obscure this fact. Technological productivity seems able to solve many of the problems by changing needs into wants; but wants isolate the individual but technology unites or at least organises them. So serious tensions are created in society. Does the PM society become politically more violent - does authority become more repressive? Certainly political reaction suggests this. Authoritarian violence creates a violent society - a criminal society. If - if - you could use organised violence to make authority less violent, you would make society less violent. But violence is not choosable in this way: it is imposed on people by the situation. Our attitudes to violence then become important because those are times when we have to legitimate violence. I think we need to understand the nature of violence - not that it's a biological accident, not that it's legitimized by the status quo, but is only legitimate when it's a response to the unbearable. The understandable should be: that terror is not a legitimate administrative means, and not even an efficient one but that there are times and places in which we cant ask people to submit to violence and exploitation. Then the terminus of violence does not matter so much. Technology imposes on us a moral responsibility to dispense with God - and so with a theological interpretation of the world. God in a technological creation is inevitably fascistic. Satyagraha in a world of needs would make sense because in it organisational problems would be anodyne: but in a world of wants it becomes dangerous because it leaves organisation (the technological, commercial, administrative world) to function independently of human judgement.

I hope these remarks are of some use. And I hope you like being back in Canada. It's a country I should like to visit. A child when it sees many snow covered mountains could well believe the sky had fallen down.

Best wishes,

Edward Bond

Max Stafford-Clark
Royal Court Theatre
London   8 March 1990

Dear Max,

My problem is an old one. Devine, as you know, thought I would never be a producible writer - though he always treated me with great courtesy and patience. It was only when I read Gaskill's book that I understood what a great strain I'd put on him (Gaskill).[1] I half suspect that he gave up the Court to escape the strain - though he is also self-destructive. I think he ran away from the real problems of the present theatre. Joint Stock was a waste - and in retrospect can be seen as destructive. It devised a method which prevented directors being properly challenged. You claim that the company was politically educated by its work on *Fanshen*. *Fanshen* is a political vulgarity - and the opportunist reactionary behaviour of David Hare recently shows that he has no political understanding; he's become an embarrassment like a child who thinks he can cleverly conceal something which is painfully obvious - I pull my school-mac over my head and vanish. Claiming to have been politicised by working with David Hare is like claiming to have been converted to christianity by the example of Judas Iscariot. I remember my shock on reading the little religious platitude you'd introduced without my permission into the programme of *Saved/Pope's Wedding* (I still get letters about it).[2] You had not understood the political seriousness of that - and so not the aesthetic seriousness. It isnt merely that in *Saved* itself there is a comment on that sort of attitude - the whole play is against it: not merely in its incentive but also in its structure and aesthetics. For me art and politics are not divisible and their connection cannot be reduced to one's own conscience. The sky has literally become political. They used to sign-write on the sky (Buy this or that). Now the debris of capitalism are covering the sky with dirt - eating at the inner texture of the sky, the structure behind the appearance. But the sky is not merely a replenishing image of poetry - it is its dynamics, as Blake and Shelley and all the rest understood. (The sky is the one thing the blind can see.) And so it becomes necessary for me to create a new aesthetics. A few

[1] Bond refers to *A Sense of Direction* by William Gaskill. London: Faber & Faber, 1989.
[2] This was a revival of *The Pope's Wedding*, directed by Max Stafford-Clark and *Saved*, directed by Danny Boyle, at the Royal Court Theatre in 1985.

years ago I saw a production of Gaskill's. It was very very very good - and utterly pointless and uninteresting, like choosing a tie for a corpse. It no longer mattered. None of it.

I think my own plays dont matter. They have no importance to me. Really I am not interested in them. It is a matter of learning how to write. But I feel this is a general problem - not one special to me. I heard one of your young assistants once telling a novice playwright how he should rewrite his play. It was disturbing to listen to because with the best of intentions it was destructive. It was putting the play into received forms, structures, norms. You find something similar in Gaskill's book when he reifies the stage's geography. Actually he talks of it as Irving might. Actors who now wish to escape from the useless work of RSC and NT directors (they're not even "good" in the RC sense) are reverting to the Irving stage - as if TV, and supermarkets and greenpeace didnt exist; as if post-Leninist politics had to be reactionary. Probably they still talk of their political commitment - but creatively they're returning to the 19th century just as Thatcher wants to return to it morally. But you can - in politics - never go back one century. The effort to do that creates a momentum which takes you back three centuries. Unfortunately this isnt so in aesthetics. Aesthetics can handle this with considerable slight of hand - which makes it more slick. A new aesthetics are necessary - a new way of writing, acting and directing and of being an audience. I was surprised how unhelpful Simon Callow's approach to acting was - it could not be used to make a production useful.[3] J[oint] S[tock] hadnt given him a new way of working. It resembled that of the actors at the RSC - though the rationale was more intelligent. That's why I left the RSC - and now McDiarmid has gone on to direct Claire Bloom in Ibsen. And Simon Callow has gone on to - I dont know what.

Just as I am not interested in my plays I dont want to direct. I'd much rather let others do it. But *Saved* at the Court was so bad you shouldnt have let it go on. Your production of *Pope's Wedding* was better - but you didnt understand the play's structure and strategy and when I tried to explain these things - and they would have excited you and you would have enjoyed using them - you would not listen. Every fortress turns into a cell: and so there is someone on the staff to tell you that the production of *Saved* was the best the Court has done. And so nothing can be learned. But if things can be learned then I wouldnt need to direct.

---

[3] Simon Callow played Lord Are in the original 1981 production of *Restoration* at the Royal Court Theatre.

Gaskill at least always listened to me very very carefully.

I wish it was all otherwise. I let the RSC do *Restoration* and didnt go near it till close to the end of the run at the Swan.[4] It was dreadful. The second half of the play had no reason to be on stage. The director couldnt bring his world to it. Restoration theatre he understood and the first part worked okay - but in the second part there was nothing. It was like the RC's latest *Saved* - emptied. I went to Newcastle and spent four days re-rehearsing the second half. Its a situation I very much dislike being in. But the play was transformed. The work I did wasnt good - I was snatching at things, manipulating them. But I knew enough about the play from working on it at the Court (not writing it) to be able to do that. The Court production had been an ordeal. It was not nice to have to try to sort out a play as complex as *Restoration* in four weeks. I remember that you said - after the rehearsal you attended - that the work was good but I did too much myself. You then gave yourself six months or something to prove to Hanif Kureshi that he couldnt write (fortunately he then proved to himself that he could). I asked the assistant you'd given me to talk about a scene: "No, she didnt talk about scenes, she just did them. Max liked to send people off and let them work on a scene and then they'd come back and show it and see if it worked." You still didnt discuss the use of the scene? "No - you showed it." Well given time I suppose you can come up with workable things - but then its like Gaskill's production - very very good and dead. I learned quickly at the RSC that you didnt ask the meaning of scenes - you just did it. But my scenes are written for *use*: not does this glove fit (ie does it work) but shall we use it for a glove or a shoe. The play doesnt decide this. Do you use the bucket of water to wash in - or put out the fire? The text: put out the fire, bathe the bride before the wedding? The discipline of theatre comes from its relationship to the street. The philosophy of a play cannot be subsumed into the play's characters. The stage has no geography. It does not relate to society as a map to a place. It is a map in which we live. That is the reality of fiction, an essential element of the human mind - and why people burn books and shoot or ignore their writers.

So that puts me in a spot. I write plays and any of them could be sent as the response to the RC commission. But you dont know how to do them. Im in

---

[4] *Restoration*, directed by Roger Michell, opened at the RSC's Swan Theatre, Stratford-upon-Avon, on 13 September, 1988. Bond subsequently re-rehearsed sections of the play in Newcastle prior to its transfer from Stratford to the Pit, Barbican Centre, London, on 29 March, 1989.

no hurry. I get such satisfaction from writing. *J[ackets] 2* is on because I was asked by Lancaster University if they could do the whole play. A schools programme in Leicester then wanted to do the second half and I said yes.[5] The working conditions are bad. You have to cast actors who'll travel to places without theatre. (At one place they thought I was Michael Bond the creator of Paddington Bear and the audience was tiny tots... they were sent away.) And although *J[ackets] 2* has been wandering around on and off since October its never been properly rehearsed. At the Bush they do half a play. The opening scenes are not made funny. They should be. I recently heard an actor (I'd worked with before) read a few lines in the canteen at the BBC - and the people around the table burst into laughter. So I know they can be funny. But I have to accept a situation where they cant be made funny. The other scenes want work on. A place like the Court could set up proper working situations for my work. But Im not going to go through the destructive process of the *Restoration* rehearsals again.

My problems are not peculiar to me. I was fortunate in that I was born into a house where there were no books. My father couldn't read - though he learned to get through a newspaper slowly, when he was about fifty. When my mother first found something I'd written she tore it up: writing was a danger to her. (They tell me secret police in other lands do the work my mother did for me: that is the difference between hegemony and tyranny.) And I grew up in very dramatic times. I think that I needed to create social language in order to hear myself. I do not write for an elite. Everything I write is very ordinary and can be understood in a very ordinary way. Then why did my mother tear up my first writings - and cry because I'd put the family in danger (and we'd been bombed night after night!...)? Because she should not have her own language. Why should I now be interested in communicating to the elite listeners - or worried about the problems of evil in the East End? Why do you Max ask so little?

I know the problems are not peculiar to me for the letters I get. So I write about the problems of aesthetics and politics to strangers. And slowly I learned what writing is. Im afraid for my society. The notion that the inevitable collapse of the super party (like the superman) has solved the problem of social living -

---

5 *Jackets II*, directed by Nick Philippou, was a touring production from the Education and Outreach Department, Haymarket Theatre, Leicester. Prior to its opening on 28 November, 1989, *Jackets II* was performed at twenty-five locations in the Midlands from 23 October until 24 November, 1989.

instead of returning it to us in new ways. What it returns to people are the processes of their own psychology - which cannot now be polarised by the fear between east and west. This makes psychology more political - not more metaphysical; the broken bricks of the berlin wall do not stop being a wall simply because they are carried away and spread far and wide in thousands of hands. The hands make them a wall. Its never been more important or more interesting to write: mistakes in writing have never been more dangerous or more ridiculous or dirtier.

It would be useful if the Court could become the place where these problems could be used. But if it cant there will be somewhere else.

Yours sincerely,

Edward

Reading and correcting this letter I see an error: I've seen more than one play directed by you - I also saw *Pope's Wedding*. And I think my remark might be misunderstood as discourteous. I dont have to see what you do: I know its very very good. I know that from the other play I saw - and from much of *P[ope's] W[edding]*. Its just that it doesnt matter anymore. It has no meaning. Like being able to play the piano when all the pianos have been destroyed. Then you are ready to begin again - because you can still read music.

EB

Ruby Cohn

London, EC4   c. 1991

Dear Ruby Cohn,

Im not sure about the final little scene of *OP*.[1] It's really using a formal
device in what is essentially a realistic play. I had in mind the scene at the end of
classical plays where a man in armour - or a burgomeister with a gold chain -
(sometimes a goddess - but was it ever a *woman*?) - appears as the representative
of morality and authority and puts everything into the (wrong) perspective. I
thought if the two people were quite naked and he "explained the universe" before
he was reincarcerated for a crime he didnt commit, that I would be able to
combine knowledge with vulnerability in an honest way. Another possibility is to
have them in bed waiting for the knock on the door - which should be heard at the
very end (no a cliche). Or perhaps at the beginning of the scene: then he begins
to talk - quite urgently? - and perhaps the knocking could be repeated more
urgently? I feel that as he is on a journey to knowledge he should be able to
speak at the end. Otherwise he is silent - like his daughter - at the fatal moment.
Why doesnt she talk at the beginning? - because she has no social language, and I
didnt want to show the resilient in-fighting of *Saved*. We now have a false
articulacy - even our spontaneity is captured. I heard some young American
tourists being interviewed on the radio about an accident they'd seen in London:
they had a microphone etiquette - a strange, convoluted language of description,
as if when they saw - and were shocked by - the event (I remember now it was an
IRA bombing) that even then their subjectivity was being produced for them.

I dont think I want to show the "interior prison" (that I use for part of the
fight between Frank and Olly) for Mike's murder of his daughter.[2] I want the
room to be very ordinary. Then there is a real prison - and then I want to put
them together and make the cell in the head: but it should be done progressively.
After the first real prison there is an "escape" into the disguised prison of Vera's
refurbished flat. After the fight between Olly and Frank - and the mental prison -
there should be the hospital cell-ward with its blind imprisoned "child." All the
rooms and boxes are stages towards the final naked scene which shouldnt "be" in
a room - there should just be a bed in a TV studio, so that the whole play becomes

---

[1] *O[lly's] P[rison]* originally written for BBC television, 1991.
[2] The "Grey Room" was not used in the BBC film.

an "escape tool," an apparatus for freedom. There is only one exterior scene: the prison yard - and this must have a high wire cage around it, and the administrative officer should be like a gold fish in solitary confinement inside his goldfish bowl - although he is obviously packing up for the night with the expectation that he will go out in freedom into his home. The "case" with its false paradise of cigarettes is also a prison. Mike opens a case after the murder but cant put the body in it: he has to take the journey of enquiry. The good room is Smiler's mother's room. Where Olly has made himself at home and which Mike enters as a weary stranger. An Oedipal reversal?

Im not sure that you're right in saying I "ascribe all such violence to capitalism." Im not sure about the "such." I certainly dont ascribe *all* violence to capitalism: people were quite violent before capitalism and there will be violence after it. I think capitalism organises violence and administers it. Physical violence is not merely reactive. The mind symbolizes its activities, which means they have meanings. Meanings cannot exist outside systems of meaning (just as you cant have one isolated letter of the alphabet, roughly) and the meanings are social. The human "meaning" is extended between the individual and society. The individual is, psychologically, that meaning and this is what he or she lives. You cannot change the meaning of the individual without changing society. Civilization is the process by which society is forced - because of its need to administer itself and its technology - to slowly understand itself. Our society is capitalist, at the moment, because it has an abundance of technology which can, partly, compensate for our failures, and also restate the problems in technological terms. There is an imbalance - and this means that the cultural (as opposed to the practical) element in the relationship can be undervalued: so our culture becomes regressive - obvious examples are urban violence, reactionary religion, the reintroduction of the death penalty in America, and so on - and I should add designer wars like the Gulf War. The relationship cannot, however, be petrified - for biological reasons: that we have to acquire language and are not born with it, that children must interpret the world before they can understand it, and so on. Even if capitalism could handle technology competently - though it cant - there would still be the cultural imperative to understand - and this is always practical and not merely theoretical or subjective: because the meaning is stretched between individual and society.

Im sorry you dont understand the *War Play* Commentary. It deals with confusions that have to be understood if we're to understand ourselves and why we need theatre - and the form that must now take if its to be a means of understanding. Because we dont understand, we misuse Beckett.

Im sorry I didnt see you at the *War Plays*. I left at the first interval because there was no point in staying to see the plays abused and the audience patronized. It's one reason why I wrote the Commentary - which you say you cannot understand.

I dont see why you should be surprised that I remember our meeting at the N[ational]T[heatre]. You remember it, why shouldnt I? You were going back to America the day after or the day after that. You'd changed your hairstyle and were wearing a slightly fuller skirt than usual, and it was as if your image was already changing because you had to go to another land: it was a little as if you were preparing to be inspected. You also stood slightly differently. You wanted me to cut out some of the priests' business (in *The Woman*) because the night before they had done it dreadfully (they had). But I didnt have to ask much of them (though they were always free to give much!) and I said I thought I had to work at it: it was necessary to the play's argument. I managed to get it better. But acting remains a problem.

Acting is now used to reproduce a subjectivity which ceased to exist forty or so years ago: a bit like the ear, which faithfully manufactures a fluid that came from the primeval sea - because we were once fish in it - although the seas have long ago changed their formula. Beckett progressively eliminates the actor because he is too fastidious to accommodate such lies - but he does not re-create. It's a bit like one of those Chinese executioners, where bits of the victim are progressively sliced away - and if the victim dies before the victim is sufficiently whittled away, then the executioner is executed. Beckett is the executioner avoiding execution.

I cannot lose my faith in theatre because that would mean losing too much contact with human beings. A young director is going to do *The Sea* at the NT later this year.[3] Im not sure I should have agreed. I saw his *Troilus and Cressida* at the RSC - it was all tricks, tricks, tricks - I looked at the audience, the earnest faces of culture. 'How can we be so abused? But he is young and it is unlikely that he is yet dead. I feel I have to talk to him and try to explain things. Behind all the trickery I suddenly had the feeling that he had himself come on stage - I could almost see him: it was as if all the flummery projected itself into the effort

---

[3] *The Sea*, directed by Sam Mendes, opened in the Lyttleton, Royal National Theatre, on 12 December, 1991.

behind it, and that *need* took almost tangible shape. His creative persona was on the stage (it doesnt often happen) and I suddenly realised it was blind. He has a blind person within him - which creates. Its that person that I can have faith in. One day that blind person *could* do the play very differently, very well, very simply - a group of actors telling the truth. He doesnt even need to "see" - perhaps his creative identity must stay blind.

Im a bit sad you dont find more in the *WP* commentary. Thanks again for your remarks.

Best wishes,

Edward Bond

Adrian Noble
Royal Shakespeare Company
London EC2   14 February 1993

Dear Adrian Noble,

Thanks for your letter. There was no need for you to apologise for its tardiness. You have been busy.

I see the point you make when you say it's always very difficult to put a value on an enterprise such as the workshops I held with Cicely Berry at the end of last year.[1] I dont agree with your "always" and "very."

I keep out of theatre politics (I am too busy with the theatre of politics to waste time on politicking) - though when confronted I try to answer truthfully, but not destructively. It isnt a secret to you that I dislike what the RSC and the other "established" theatres (including the Court) now do. I disliked your *Winter's Tale* because it was anti-Shakespeare.[2] Worse, it was successful. The audience enjoyed themselves because Shakespeare (even mangled) has more life than most dramatists. And there is always the pleasure of watching accomplished actors. But the structure of the play was destroyed. The country scenes are immediate in their appeal (certainly in your production). But the play creates a tension between the dark world and a world where the unbearable is made bearable by and changed by the characters' ability to endure. It isnt flatly a contrast between court and country: the country is a place of trade and other forms of theft. Which is the disaster and which the echo, which the fire and which its reflection in the clouds? - is not the point. You can say that the fire is ignited by its reflection. It is through the politics of the rural scenes - in their trade and psychology - that the miracle at the end is accomplished: made plausible if not real. And in the darkness, hope need only be plausible: this will incite the resources of the psyche and daily life. In this way Shakespeare makes a map of our place in the world.

None of this is approached in your production. Instead, you give us a good time. It is the duty of art to make us happy - but what is happiness? Art has always been like the orchestra in Auschwitz. Why did Michelangelo, and the rest

---

[1] Edward Bond and Cicely Berry held three weeks of workshops with nine RSC actors at The Other Place, Stratford-upon-Avon, 16 November - 4 December, 1992.
[2] Bond refers to the 1992/3 season at the Royal Shakespeare Company.

of them, have to paint hell? Or Dante go there? Or Cervantes? Or Tolstoy? Or the Greeks? Or Goya? Or Mozart? Or Shakespeare? Because you are not human if you do not encompass the extremes of human experience.

Your *WT* abandons the extremes for pleasure - and so misses the great happiness of the play. Easy rides dont take us on long journeys. On its chosen ground your production seemed to me much better than much of what I saw at Stratford: though Peter Hall had a streets-ahead advantage over you because he did (more or less) the whole play - and so *All's Well* worked in a way that your *WT* never could. Shakespeare is a better adaptor than you.

It seemed to me that the RSC productions I saw were handling out effects and ignoring causes. Each production lit, acted, dressed in the same way. I waited for the music (it seemed to be the same in each production) to sound at the same time underlining the same emotion. Difference in emotion, music, staging was only a difference in fast and slow, soft and loud, brighter and duller. There was no analysis of any situation and so no meaning: and so the imagination was never released from its prisons. (Strobe lighting is merely the reflections of the imagination imprisoned in a treadmill.)

I dont want an austere theatre. I want a theatre with imagination and meaning. That's why societies have theatres - to enable imagination to take the journeys reason will have to take. To go to tragic darkness because there we learn to imagine light. The Greeks went so far as to say on their stage: "It's better never to have been born, but if that disaster were to befall you it is better to die quickly." They then said "hurray" and went rejoicing down into their city. Unless we have the sense and strength to do the thing equivalent to our age, we become not even entertainers but mere distractors. There is no alternative to this.

So our theatre doesnt examine anymore - and the audience is debased. There is a clear connection between Jacobean theatre and our theatre. At the end of *The Changeling* the father stands on stage.[3] A few feet from him his daughter is murdered. A madhouse keeper, inmates, fakers, and others watch. What does the father do? You dont find incidents such as this in Ibsen (not even in *When We Dead Awaken*), Chekhov, not even in Strindberg. Yet isnt it just the sort of incident that could occur in a modern play? In the Stratford production the father did nothing (nothing!). How do you find out what he does? Stanislavsky wont help you. Brecht gets nearer - he says "observe." Stanislavsky says "feel." But

[3] *The Changeling*, by Middleton and Rowley, was in the 1992/3 season of the Royal Shakespeare Company.

you have no precedents to base the feeling on. There are no situations like this. Except that we have all been in them. They are in the world of our imagination. Really there. And justified in being there. The answer doesnt lie in merely reproducing the imagination. But in placing it in the tensions of the real event. The two together make theatre and always have done. There is no other form of theatre that fulfills the need that makes societies create theatre. The December workshops were largely based on giving actors access to their imagination: in its psychological and bodily prison. But then we need to relate the imaginative to the reasoned: what we find in the imagination has no use - use is a further stage. Then reason and imagination become processes of accesses to each other's power.

Our theatre needs quite fundamental work on these problems. It is very easy to pretend it doesnt. Consumption satisfies for a time, tastes can be multiplied and appetites can even be instructed - but I cant honestly say our theatre is producing a nouvelle cuisine: unless it is creative in the way I've described theatre is always cannibalism - and the most that could be hoped for would be nouvelle cannibalism.

I think that if you look at the work of some contemporary dramatists and compare that with contemporary productions, it might not be so difficult to see the value of the December workshops. To me they are something of a distraction because of course I would rather be writing. But then who will produce what I write? Or produce the work of other, newer writers? You will remember the history of my association with the RSC. It sank to its lowest when I had to go to Newcastle and re-rehearse the second half of *Restoration*. It was necessary to do that not because I had some secrets but because the director wasnt adequately equipped. How could he be? We write in new ways and no one has radically asked why and how. The present RSC is anti-Shakespeare and so it must be anti-modern. I hope this remark wont seem unsympathetic. Running the RSC must be demanding work. You must be busy - perhaps it will be helpful if you listen to someone like me?

Everyone at T[he] O[ther] P[lace] was very kind and helpful to me. I told you that I needed a month at the least, and I got three weeks. And so you knew I could not in that time do adequate work. Perhaps we missed something. Even so, I was stimulated by the inventiveness of the actors. I think it would be good if I did more work at the RSC.

I am not someone who hawks his wares in the hopes of finding a buyer. If you feel a need for a writer like me at the RSC perhaps you could define it a little.

And suggest how that need could be met. But you would have to know the need before I could see sense in giving up writing time.

A man ran a race. So keen was he on winning that he won: he burst through the tape first. But when he went to be given his prize and reached out his hands to take it, he toppled over. It was then that he saw that he had only one leg. This is a difficult story from the imagination when it reaches the real.

Yours sincerely (and good luck in your new season),

Edward Bond

Adrian Noble
Royal Shakespeare Company
Stratford-upon-Avon
Warwickshire CV7 6BB   21 March 1993

Dear Adrian Noble,

Thanks for your letter. I dont want to say too much about your production
of *W[inter's] T[ale]*.[1] I agree with much of what you say about W[illiam]
S[hakespeare]. Of course he is dealing with "one world." You then have to say
why he deals with it the way he does. Why are there the divisions between court
and country in *WT*? Why is *WT* full of paradoxes, conflicts, reality annealed by
magic, politics made bearable by myth? The paradoxes are not there for artistic
reasons, for the pleasure they give. They come from the tensions of WS's time.
The monarchical order he relied on was swept away in the lifetime of his
children: his house was used to quarter the armies of regicides and theatre-closers;
his myths were demonized and became chancres not healings. The fault of your
WT was that it glossed these tragic tensions and made them benign and trivial
without exposing them. This made the audience happy - but it didnt give them
the deeper joy WS evokes to reconcile the irreconcilable: his joy is utopian, and
exists in its failure. If stones could speak, and statues move?
    There is another important point. WS's political order was also a moral
one. The rectified political state was a moral order, the earthly counterpart of the
city of God.   Thus psychology and politics become one.   Hamlet is the
psychological centre of the state. The state is expressed through his psyche. The
tragic solution of his psyche's problems becomes the beneficent solutions of the
state's problems. It's a world view that the industrial revolution made obsolete:
and so the regicides take up quarters in New Place. The state can no longer be
represented (dramatically) by the psyche of its ruler. Oedipus has become one of
the chorus, Hamlet one of Fortinbras's troops. A modern writer deals with the
same problems - the relation between individual and society, between the psyche's
need to imagine reality, and technology's practice of changing reality - that WS
had to deal with; but of course our answers are different. As God is dead the state
is not his moral order and cannot be changed through the processes of the psyche.

---

[1] Adrian Noble's production of *The Winter's Tale* is discussed in the previous letter.

No writer was more political than WS. But a modern writer has to just about reverse WS's political procedures in order to reach the same political realities in their modern form. Doing that releases the drama inherent in our lives; the many-sided relationship between authority and the individual is the basic substance of drama, and the mind is itself a dramatic structure because it is always negotiating this relationship and drama is structured into it to enable it to do so. It is why we have theatres - and why the boundary between sanity and madness is blurred, the space between happiness and unhappiness so small, and the journey between childhood and age so full of visions. Art is a land we cannot reach because it does not exist, but we can throw bits of reality at it.

You say you revealed the true structure of WS in a way you havent seen before. That may be - but of course it could still be saying very little... I think it, and your defence of it, seriously discount WS's real, late problem. But I think you can do this with WS and still produce something. If you do it to a modern play you produce rubbish, and perhaps the playwright will have obliged by already writing rubbish for you. The way you approached *WT* was the way the RSC approached my *Restoration* - and you saw the results. This isnt a personal grudge. It's widely recognised that the theatre has become useless in dealing with our own times. You must hear this almost constantly. No dramatist seriously dealing with our problems could have been content with your production of *WT*. Remember I wrote about the *WT* because it was about the most accomplished production I saw at Stratford. We visit a classical ruin in a very sophisticated way. We dont go there with an estate agent wondering if we can still live in it. But we go to a revival of a classical play in order to live with it, to make it useable again - to make it pertinent and problematic. Your *WT* teaches us very bad lessons about our life. It is anti-Shakespeare and so anti-modern. Why is it commonly accepted that our theatre has lost touch with our times? - is anti-modern? Because our theatres try to do with modern plays what they - you and others - do with Shakespeare. They cant do this. Modern problems are urgent and cannot be glossed, cannot be reduced to benign solutions (your *WT*) or reified in reductive pathology in the way *Tamberlaine* was. An audience giggling at the terrors of *Tamberlaine*? - and the last fifteen minutes of the production might have been acceptable on the second day of rehearsals but not later.

To be anti-Shakespearean is to be anti-modern and vice versa. Does this statement disturb you? You will not do Shakespeare well till you can do modern plays well. The problem for modern theatre is that it cant accommodate writers.

TV has writing-teams and a few privileged writers - such as Potter - who are really embarrassing in their triviality. The Court for a time solved this problem - much to Devine's surprise (he thought the solution would be different). The Court fell apart through the squabbles of its directors - the writers (though writing differently) didnt squabble. Gaskill then made the mistake of founding Joint Stock - trying to subordinate the writer directly to the director. It failed. The writer has to set problems not provide solutions. Directors now cant learn the way of solving the problems of modern plays. I hear this constantly from young writers. We need a new sort of acting and a new way of using the stage. I've written about this at length and need not repeat it here.

You stress the importance of involving actors and designers in the creation of a production. Of course that's important - and your actors enjoyed working on the rural parts of *WT*. But in general I found, at Stratford, that the actors felt exploited and misused, not fully involved in what they were asked to do, not allowed to confront the play. You'll know that I share your views about involvement. Then why was the design at Stratford so repetitious, the acting so uniform and mechanical? You had to look at your programme to see what play you were at. I suppose that sounds rude? - but how else to convey what I saw?

The December workshops showed me again that there was a need for a new approach and that it was possible. But what we did merely vanishes in the general wash. There's no point in me repeating that. Perhaps there could be a production? Perhaps some sort of unit could be created that had responsibility for modern plays? Perhaps there could be series of workshops based on modern plays?

I suppose I sound critical but I dont give a damn. The matter is too important to avoid stepping on toes if they're in the way. You cant be as satisfied with your work as you say? You'd have to be very silly to be that. Cezanne took his canvases home and stamped on them, Michelangelo hacked at his last statues in despair, the Mona Lisa smiles because she knows she's looking at someone who cant paint. Your final phrase about "not bothering" is defensive and silly. I acknowledge what you do but tell you it isnt enough, that you waste your ability and the opportunities of your position. Really I say these things not for myself - Im already too busy and have too little time to write - but because I want younger writers to have their place - I want the excitement of their theatre. Nothing is more soul-destroying than a theatre which is satisfied when it shouldnt be or an audience that applauds when it's been cheated. If you share my need, then you'll take steps so that you and I can meet it. But I need to know that you have some sympathy with the ideas I've described. Otherwise it's useless my coming to Stratford. The world is too interesting to waste time being shown round it by a medieval estate agent. So what shall we do?

Yours sincerely,

Edward Bond

Index

Other titles in the Contemporary Theatre Studies series

This book is part of a series. The publisher will accept continuation orders which may be cancelled at any time and which provide for automatic billing and shipping of each title in the series upon publication. Please write for details.